DONALD GARDNER

NEW AND SELECTED POEMS
1966–2020

PHOTO BY AMINA MARIX EVANS

Donald Gardner

New and Selected Poems

1966–2020

Grey Suit Editions

First published in 2021 by
Grey Suit Editions, an affiliate
of Phoenix Publishing House Ltd

British Library Cataloguing in Publication Data
A C.I.P. catalogue record for this book is available
from the British Library

Paperback ISBN: 978-1-903006-25-2
e-book ISBN: 978-1-903006-26-9

Designed and typeset in Monotype Bembo by Anvil

Printed and bound in the United Kingdom
by Hobbs the Printers Ltd

Grey Suit Editions
33 Holcombe Road, London N17 9AS
https://greysuiteditions.co.uk/

for Selese

CONTENTS

from *The Wolf Inside* (2014)

from *Early Morning* (2017)

New Poems (2017–2020)

Early Poems

IN MEXICO CITY

Packed in a taxi like luggage
uncomfortable
like someone getting ready for Munich
how can I tell the driver

I am not a gringo?
I want to apologize
for Vietnam
but not pay more than five pesos

or miss my bus
or dare those faces
out of the starving tenements,
a bad man plagued by time.

But taking a sudden corner
I give the driver all my change
and am not longer English or American.
I am the rain that beats my face.

IN VILLAHERMOSA

In Villahermosa
there were three monkeys
in a cage like slaves
but with wildly lyrical tails.

And one of them came up to me
hugging his mouth
perhaps to stop laughing.
And though I have travelled a long way

I have never shaken hands with a monkey.
And this one
had fingers like a pianist
but was much more gentle.

And when he patted me on the head
he might have been a priest
if he hadn't lolloped away to pee.
Why that's my hypocrite brother.

MAN IN DISTORTING MIRROR

He keeps his distance with affection and
Works out his multiself by long division.

By these lights, children, Quixote and Byron join –
The gothic stagger in a velvet curtain,
The cloud-capped Don puts on a certain swagger.

Watch him, this hero of barbecues and beanfeasts,
Clumsy with spoons, preferring fists and jaws.

A firelight banqueteer, lord among ladies,
Basking in many voices of his own.

And his best trumpet is his honking nose –
Sure, he's inflated as a shepherd's bagpipes,
His majesty's a double-barrelled name.

Soft hints impinge upon his bloated image,
A pin may spoil his perfect seamless belly.

Bring music on to soothe his cabbage ear,
'Eh what?' he says, 'repeat that dying fall.'

His glad rags droop like leaves, poor chanticleer,
Quixote and Byron joined dissolve in Pierrot,
Sharing a joke but only with himself.

Call for those cartoon nudes whose every inch
Dripped sense and incense on his roving eye,

Whose lewd unravelling of dainty limbs,
So cunningly displayed, once led his dance.

All gone – their fragrant laughter vanishing
Leaves him alone, a monster in the maze
Pouncing on strands of wool for some way out.

And his enormous hands are sad and empty,
Look, there is need of much affection here.

His gamin smile, sheep's look and two gauche eyes
Make distance seem a trickery of optics,
And this compels the watcher's gaze until

With one engaging yawn the mirror-self
Catches him unawares and eats him whole.

THE BOYS OF KENNINGTON SCHOOL

Some of them come out of Hieronymus Bosch and go
    back there.
One of them has climbed into his desk and is rowing it
    slowly forward.
Two of them are embracing or fighting and work their
    way right through each other and out again.
Three of them are putting a triangular set square on a
    fourth boy's head so that it will stay with him, an
    odd mark for life.
Four of them beg me to send them to the headmaster to
    be beaten and five plead with me not to send them.
One of them must be doing something wrong so I beat
    myself.
Most of them go to the lavatory and come back having
    masturbated looking strangely thoughtful, their
    heads spinning slowly.
All of them don't know anything at all hardly.
The law of the land requires all children to go to school.
Thank God there's a law – otherwise how would they
    all have got here?

from
Peace Feelers
(1969)

PASSAVIA

'Passavia' means roughly 'keep moving', so
this dog got called Passavia by
the foreign painters who lived in Anticole
because most of them didn't know any Italian
and the locals never said anything to it but:
'passa via, passa via, passa via'.

Like name like nature, always
                              on the move at
4 or 5 miles an hour
                      up across down
flights of steps round
                        and back again past
where they kept the donkeys locked up for the night –
useful animals, donkeys.

Licked up dirty puddle water and the foreigners
took to the animal feeding it on
prime chop-steak, but
it didn't get any ideas above its station, or
if the bitches were anything to go by,
didn't have much of a station, never
humped any of them, maybe hadn't been
taught about humping; or hunting –
not its line either – it would follow the hunters
at a safe distance sometimes
but didn't seem interested in actually catching anything; it
must have lacked motivation; it was
a weird dog. It couldn't bark.

No station so
       kept moving,
no motivation so
       kept moving, an
irrational animal
       kept moving by
'passa via' said
       more or less in its direction
or by a boot
       in its direction
kept moving.

(Very rarely across the open sunlit piazza of the village
but alongside the cold shoulders of houses,
an elongated trotting shadow.)

And it was a blurred animal,
black and white spotted, only
more blurred as it got
older or moved faster, and pink
round the mouth, mild pink eyes and patches
of pink where the skin had worn out
and – between the toes – red; and it
gravitated towards the foreigners,
followed them when they got off the bus –
had that much of an instinct
for its own kind – would take
what they gave it without
saying anything, but could sit for hours
being an artist's model –
only time it seemed to sit anywhere,

because Passavia
was its name
                    now travelling the
other side of nowhere since
                              one fine day
when they hadn't anything to do,
                              the villagers
stoned it to death
                    and went and told Ida
who told me this story
                    four years later.

NIGHT THOUGHTS

i

Each night before I go to sleep I put on my thickest sweater, my climbing boots and snow goggles, because I don't know where I am going – maybe to climb Mount Everest from the Chinese side.

ii

My wife wears a red polka-dot bikini and carries a parasol because she believes in a different kind of trip, wanting the creamy edges of the Pacific breakers to make the round tour of her beautiful salty body.

iii

Once I bought her some climbing clothes and persuaded her to wear them. We both sweltered together under the noonday sun. A restless night. Next morning she said to me as tactfully as possible: 'what did I tell you?' I have to admit she is nearly always right.

iv

Sometimes I take off my crampons, lay my ice-axe neatly by the side of my bed, take off my woolly mittens, wipe the sun-cream off my cheeks with a face-cloth, take off my windbreaker and heavy sweater, take off my cord trousers and long underpants, take off my check shirt and string vest, say hello to my St. Christopher medal and slip it under the bed. My wife is very nice about it and says that ritual is an important element in love-making.

v

I am lonely among these snows. I am sick of the Chinese
side. In my sleep I am apolitical. I am lonely with nothing to
love but my ice-axe. I am lonely with my sense of humour.
The wind roars round the North Col like an express train
permanently derailing itself, so loud that even if I tried
shouting, she wouldn't hear me on her South Sea island.
Half way across the world the wind is drowned in the roar
of the Pacific breakers and when I wake for a moment, I am
amazed to see that she is sleeping peacefully and smiling.

CLIMBING THE EIGER IN OUR SLEEP

Last night
        sleeping together, our heads
on the same pillow,
           our bodies
at an angle to each other
             we looked
like a pair of sycamore wings
              and woke at 2 a.m.
not believing
        it could be so early
and dreaming half-awake –
           our head so close – we had
drawn the same dream
           from a common pool –
yes, but a terrifying dream
          of separation.

And we couldn't
        put the dream together
again; only
        in the cold light I write in
this morning
        I think maybe it was the one
of climbing the North
        Face of the Eiger,
bitter runnels the sleet
        fills and spills through
the only finger-holds
        slipping through my fingers

which I find when I wake
                    are reaching for
the soft notches of your backbone
                              you've turned towards me
turning to the wall
                    of our room that turns
to the same North Face
                         in your dream with no
finger-holds you can talk to.

And I am strangely
                    held by the dream
so that I listen to you
                    only grudgingly,
grudgingly admit
                    the feel of your
toe on the
              sole of my foot and my finger
tracing your groin
                    and later the fumbling of
late-night love-making
                         clinging
to each other
              like swimmers
drowning or
              treading water
for the time being
                    reassuring ourselves we're
together again
              only to
roll over afterwards and
                    crash away blindly from each other

into the blizzard we sleep in
                    and wake in the morning

two heads on
            the same pillow,
sycamore wings
                fallen from a high tree
in Autumn.

Tree or pool – these
                   arbitrary images we
clutch at like finger-holds
                     to explain
how the surface of the
                   mirror is
only the surface,
               how no mirror
is deep enough
               to find ourselves in,
how the other
             side of the mirror
we are only the size of
                  the finger-holds
we clutch at and lose,
                 how mirrors
are empty
         if we only
leave them alone for a moment.

We drew from the same pool
                  last night

unity in
        separation –
beyond it, beyond us,
            the strictest neutrality –

and are gentler
        not wiser this morning,
my toe sliding against
          the sole of your foot,
your finger
       tracing my groin,
this July morning
        with its grey skies
with its wind
       like a premature Autumn.

INDIRECTIONS

The telephone rang while I was washing my hair
and getting out of the bath I misjudged the height and fell
on my right side (not the side I sleep on, thank god!)
and thought I'd broken at least a hip
and lay there grunting to myself like a piece of bad rhetoric
or that whale the seventeenth-century Hollanders admired
    so much,
washed up on the beach at Scheveningen for all to see.
Nobody listens to rhetoric but you can't ignore a whale;
so I thought I'd make a poem of it, telling myself
beauty is truth but ugliness means well.
The phone stopped ringing and maybe I'd missed a date
    with love
and broken my right hip into the bargain
but it's not the side I sleep on and there are other times
and if I'd got there with all that water on me
I'd probably have been electrocuted dead.
You learn to take things slowly or fall flat.

THE TRUTH OF VULTURES

'I worry just as much about the injured kids as the next fellow – maybe more so'. Chester L. Cooper, an official of the State Department in Washington.

(Ramparts Magazine, January 1967)

I remember in San Carlos, Nicaragua, last Fall, seeing two
vultures perched on roof-trees like strangers exacting
tribute of the town. Black hooded vultures in total
agreement over what is truth.
And I remember the fat army cops of San Carlos who taxed
the 15-year old kid 5 pesos for permission to row his
boat out of dock,
and I see a photo of Dean Rusk and McNamara in the New
York Times, March 2nd, declaring total agreement;
and I wonder if an analogy is fair and whether an agreement
between two vultures is fair
and what the vultures can have had in common and if their
agreement was good or for the common good;
and I wonder if there is an analogy to be made between
McNamara and a vulture and if Dean Rusk has
anything in common with a small-town bully;
and whether in fact McNamara and Dean Rusk ever
honestly disagree on anything and whether there is a
basis for an agreement between the vultures of
Nicaragua and the Pentagon – maybe for a mopping-up
operation,
and whether the vultures though somewhat homespun
wouldn't make a cleaner job of it than napalm and
phosphorus
and I wonder what the kid with the rowboat felt about

paying 5 pesos and whether they would have put him
    in jail if he hadn't paid and what he meant when he
    called the cop a 'pendejo';
and I wonder if there is a configuration of the stars that
    sanctions our operations in South-East Asia
and whether there is an absolute truth in the operation
    of vultures,
or in operation Black-Eye when 50,000 black eyes were
    printed in Saigon by USIS and planted in the huts of
    murdered VC;
and I wonder if I worry as much as Chester L. Cooper or
    more so and whether worry can be counted like money
    and what happens to all the worry.
And I thirst for the great doll-mender who could take all
    these ragged edges of worry and stitch them together
    in a haphazard patchwork quilt for all the children we
    have murdered by accident,
and I wonder if there is another truth besides the truth
    of vultures;
and my mind prowls around the base of trees in Vietnam
    where they have strapped the VC prisoners to stop
    them escaping and I wonder if they can tell me but
    they are silent,
and it goes back to Tompkins Square where Skaggs's Christ
    has been standing since the beginning of time;
and it is a red-grey angry evening after snowfall and I
    cannot see through the dark what he is thinking –
whether he is weeping or yawning but I think maybe he is
    winking at me,
and that perhaps there is another kind of truth and that
    the vultures
don't have the monopoly.

BREAD AND STONES

I come into London with nothing to do and no money.
I sit on a bench with two tramps. We smoke butt-ends.
One of them talks about the freedom of the individual and
    the other
about the lost glories of the British Empire. Sunset glories.
The sun falls away like an old Woodbine
but Battersea power station is still smoking.
I like the freedom of the individual, my life to live;
and the tramps hardly think of rifling my pockets.
Hardly surprising, though I look the next morning
as though I had come from a late-night party; my bow tie
is crestfallen and my blue suit wears its stains lightly like
    an empty wallet.
I tell them I used to be a trombonist but am out of work.
    Not true.
I have been working busily through the night, my head
    full of skyscrapers,
projects for the ideal city, an empire of the mind
where Plato is vastly entertained by Brigitte Bardot and
    St. Francis loosens his girdle,
and I have never played the trombone and the tramps
    know it
though one of them says I would make an excellent
    panhandler.
My head is still full of skyscrapers though I have never
    been to New York.
I'd like best of all to build a project modelled on Assisi as
    seen from Perugia,
catching the sunlight at every angle every hour of the day,
angles for angels to house the very old,

those who talk to themselves in their sleep or pick their
    noses,
those whose bodies are too heavy for them to bear, whose
    children are bored with them.
We would have dances on Saturday in the main piazza
and tell old jokes about old times. We remember St. Francis
when he was just a wild broth of a boy before the birds
    got him.
But it is morning and the cops are moving us on.
In London they are the one surviving national monument.
That's what happens to you when you lose and empire.
And the tramps pretend not to know me – so much for
    freedom of the individual.
And I move on and my project is, to say the least,
    unfinished.

from
For the Flames
(1974)

FOR THE FLAMES

In the matter of travelling light I think that these men are
    exemplary.
They must have whittled their lives down to an ultimate
    simplicity,
clean as a white bone polished by the sea. They have moved
    on a stage ahead of us.
They have dropped a long line into empty space and found
    it anchored
a little way beyond all dialectics and metaphysics.
Buddhist, Christian and Marxist are drawn here to the same
    elementary conclusion.
I think it is a simple voice that speaks to us out of these
    flames.

I think it is like a clean white bone stuck in the throat of
    governments.
It speaks to us in the interstices between civilizations.
The horror stories in the afternoon editions are of a
    completely different order.
The roar of burning kerosene becomes here almost an
    incidental accompaniment
and the hot wind from these flames shouldn't make us shy
    of coming closer
and listening with an ear tuned in to the other side of
    silence.
I think it is a voiceless voice that speaks to us out of these
    flames.

It is a voice that speaks like the silence of lovers late at
    night

when words are left behind and only their thoughts engage
in tender argument
slipping around each other like little fishes. Wherever it
comes from,
from Wenceslaus Square, from a broken crossroads in Saigon
or opposite the lighted window where McNamara worked
late,
they speak to us here as well, man to woman, man to man.
Human speech is restored to us out of these flames.

It is the persistency of water wearing away rock.
It is the persistency of roots breaking through concrete.
It is slow and certain as cumulo-nimbus clouds gathering
wetness.
It is a heavy raincloud risen from the brows of starving
peoples.
It speaks to us out of all the myths we have ever known:
the hero surrounded by enemies who put on his cloak
called Invisible,
and the tale of the child sleeping peacefully adrift on a
great ocean.

It is the voice of a few people with exceptional daring.
Magically they have become part of the air which
surrounds us.
It takes our breath away. It gives our breath back to us.
It throws the question back at us: who are we?
It elevates us to where we are, to a high windswept plateau,
hungry for love. crying for home, naked in a world gone
mad.

It is a hard voice brought to us on a bitter wind in a bitter
    time,
hammering home the necessity of our exile.
It is the most enduring voice I have ever heard.

TO BRECHT

'What times are these
when a conversation about trees seems almost a crime.
Because it includes a silence about so many misdeeds!'

It's like this, Brecht.
The end of the world
is going on behind my
shoulders as I write.

I am trying
to describe
this one flower.

I have never
been so much in love
with gardens.

The lighting's gone
                but
the flames of the apocalypse
mean I can work
by night too.

I am doing my best
against odds
to preserve something.

THE ROAD SOUTH, EDINBURGH
TO LONDON

i

Whether we go south or north
is unimportant.
This is a small country.

You can roll it up like a map,
put it in your bluejeans pocket
or hang it on a line to dry.

It is studded with sad-eyed student poets
coming on like they're Gary Snyder.
The woods are full of them.
They leave their picnic litter of
stoned zen lyrics written in
desperate circumstances in
single bedsits in Sheffield, Doncaster, Derby.

There's not room in the country for all this poetry.
There's not room in the country for all this stoned
        earnestness.

Because there's no room they become terribly earnest.
Because there's no room, a terrible inwardness.

ii

I want the poem to dictate
as the road dictates
our direction.

I want the poem
that says north
where it reads south.

I want the poem
with such a high frequency of inwardness
when it explodes the country goes up too.

I want it to
burn out the barrier
between the imaginary and the so-called real.

Since I could see I
haven't been able to
see any difference.

All my so-called education
having been a bone-headed skull-bashing conspiracy
to separate me from my real self

which is the imagination
renewing itself through action,
total energy of a man making himself free.

And if I work now roughly 9 to 5 writing poems
it's to undo the threads that others tie.

I want the poem
to undo all do.

I want the poem
that undoes me.

I want to be
the road I ride.

To die as I.

   iii

The reason there's no room in the country, Mister Powell,
is nothing to do with the immigrants.

The reason is ½% of the population
owning 90% of the wealth.

The reason is 700 years of laws
and the police to enforce them.

The reason you think that immigrants are noisy
is that this country has a low tolerance level to noise.
In other words, it's no longer safe
for anybody alive to live in.

Still, I see what you mean, Mister Powell:
even if the whole structure were to cave in on us
(and it will)
there'd still be four mad old army colonels and the colonels'
    ladies
playing bridge in a drawing-room in Aldershot
not noticing that anything has happened
(and they don't).

There's an old zen riddle, Mister Powell:
does the banner wobble or the wind?

Mister Powell, your mind wobbles.

Mine boggles.

The reason there's no room in this country
is that everyone's stopped breathing,
so they get uptight inside
and blame the inside on the outside.

iv

Staying still is also some journey.
We are standing by the A1 on the edge of Edinburgh
eating the fruit you bought.
I spill a polythene bag of nuts and raisins on the road.
You pick them up and feed them to both of us.
We are travelling.

Obviously I 'love' you.
It doesn't matter whether or not we are lovers for this story.
I don't know what the word 'love' means.
The point of this story is somewhere else:

The experience of eating nuts and raisins off the road.
The way the bag exploded when I tried to open it.
The experience of the road and the tarmac slightly
        softening in the heat.

The sudden whiteness of the heat.
The absence of thought.
No need to travel.
We are travelling.

And a month back I rode my Honda across London to
    Kew on a Bank Holiday
through the holiday traffic, the heat, the exhaust
and saw nothing because of the holiday crowds and the
    fact that there was too much to see and all of it
    crowded into greenhouses
and I might as well have been back where I spent the
    morning in what passed for a garden in the house
    I used to live in in Islington:
just a few slabs of concrete and nothing to see but the sky.

You don't need anything but the sky over your head
and yourself transparent as the sky.

There is no point to this story.
There is no story.

We are there.

LET'S ALL MAKE LOVE TONITE IN LONDON

The soft contours.
The rounded miniature hills.
The toy buses.
The soft soap of the politicians
and a soft centre to the language.
The 4-syllable explanations
in the pages of the New Statesman or the Guardian.
Boys' boarding schools, bad plumbing, the accent on virtue.
The homey nostalgia of days in early Autumn.
The blasé accents.
The rich widows of Kensington.
The letters to the Times.
The counting of small change
in cash-registers in little groceries in Holloway, Finsbury
    or Camden.
100,000 foreign students who don't know anyone.
The waiting for something to happen.
The fear of anything new.
The division into classes and of houses into bed-sitting
    rooms.
The rich of the rich and the poor of the poor.
The loneliness of long-distance spinster schoolteachers.
400 miles of middle-income housing.
Dogs, cats, women with push-chairs, squalling babies.
Burnt toast. Indian tea, transport cafés, families,
family quarrels, family reunions and Christmas
like a pink bow tied round the throat of the year.
Sick relatives, social justice, the doctrine of work, landlords.

A prurient press, The Queen and the Queen Mother,
Prince Philip, Prince Charles and all the Royal Family.

England,
October 1969.
Or any other year you care to mention.

A GUIDE TO GREECE, 1970

These are the Greek people vanished behind their faces.
These are the olive groves cancelled till further notice.
Here is Mount Hymettos. It has become invisible.
This is a stone life-size copy of the Parthenon.
This is the country. Don't ask where the jails are.
This is Bouboulinos street winding round and round the
    country.

This is the rough Greek wine. It tastes of water.
This is the water. It tastes of air.
This is the air. It tastes of nothing.
Where is your hotel with its air-conditioning?
Don't ask a policeman: this is collaboration.
Here are two lovers with a policeman watching.

This is the language. Empty like a plague city.
This is Athens. Nobody lives here.
This is the language. You can learn it in a second.
This is the language: shouts when a man is beaten.
This is the language: screams when a man is tortured.
This is the language: weeps when a man is murdered.
This is the poet of the language. Yannis Ritsos. 61. In prison.
    On Samos. Coughing blood.
Here are the tourists taking photos of each other.

from
No Flowers for the Man-Made Desert
(1985)

I DANCE WITH A HERO OF OUR TIME

I dreamed I was dancing with one of the first astronauts. He whirled me round and round the ballroom floor. In his bulging foam-rubber arms I felt protected. But when I saw the empty expression on his face, philosophic doubt invaded my centres – you've guessed it – like a gang of businesslike Martians determined to search and destroy.

That face had seen too much emptiness. Staring at the night sky was no different from some lonesome bar-propper gazing at the bad taste wallpaper behind the barman's ear.

'John G-Glenn', I heard myself whispering, 'd-do you think maybe our world, I don't mean just our g-globe world, yes, that t-t-too, but our c-c-conceptual w-w-world, all our paradise of thought and ideas, might just be a fantasy of our overheated brains?'

'Don't worry, sonny', he answered me reassuringly, as he turned his handsome profile towards me looking into the future. 'I've been up there and I know it all and I'm telling you, it's good, it's all good. There's a plan behind it all, I promise you. Intellectual doubt', he went on, 'sure, that ain't no sin. Only if you're troubled by doubt, just take some time out with yourself, all on your own, and spin off into orbit till you've figured it out. Maybe you'll come back and maybe you won't. 'Cause there's casualties to doubt just like there are in my line of business. All you have to do is to hold on tight and, above all, don't worry.'

So saying he picked me up and whirled me round and round and round. John Glenn, that was – while the music played as if it meant to go on for ever. How pleasant it was to have a mind empty of fears, even if by the same token, it was also empty of ideas. For while the dream lasted my doubts were indeed stilled and my mind went blank. Blank as any piece of empty space, blank even as the ideational void that I filled with this poem. Just words, as they say.

THE FINEST HOUSING DEPARTMENT

You are sitting at the desk of a housing official,
and it is words she talks, she has the words.
Her tone is one of sweetest reason
but the words, the words, they seem to fade in air.
She tells you she wishes she could help you
and her good intentions make you both feel good
and the way her tongue falls makes you feel helped already
and indeed you are helped – to a cup of hot coffee! –
as you sit there in your leaking boots and steaming anorak.
She is one of the new generation of functionaries,
so different from the crabbed old pen-scratchers of the
        tradition
you'd hardly imagine it was the same job they were both
        doing.
She is one where you feel the menthol on her breath as
        she strides close to you
to read your record on the computer screen.
That flash of thigh you see in the slit of her gold-belted
        short black dress –
did that get browned on Crete this summer?
She certainly looks like she was off to slay some minotaur
in the echoing halls of interconnecting departments.
(In your mind everything gets jumbled as though you
        had no walls between ideas!)
How kindly she tells you she cannot help you directly
but that she will be glad to give you a form to take to show
        to another department!
And her accent falls on each syllable calmly
like a seagull landing on a frozen canal.

And the unfaltering play she makes of carefully selected
    sentences,
coupled with the hissing damp outside and the airless
    comfort of that centrally heated office,
sends you into a sort of pleasurable swoon.
Only when you are back on the street clasping a form
    and still homeless
does a certain basic despair set in
that even the finest housing department could not cure,
tinged as it is with those metaphysical askings
that marvellously lend bureaucracy a symbolic function,
    as Franz Kafka knew.
Or as we used to sing at school,
'God moves in a mysterious way . . .':
thin treble voices lifted in empty praise.

from
Starting from Tomorrow
(1995)

CAP ON MY HEAD

With my ego that moved like a house
and my id like a snail inside,
I knew how to get my own way.
No wonder my mum was afraid.

She gave me the best of her youth
but the best is never enough.
She cried in the sink half the night,
so I was sent to a school in the south.

Where the terrible sea roars in,
my knee-caps were chafed and red.
Where the cabbage fields sigh in the wind,
a cap was shoved down on my head.

Thoroughly licked into shape,
now I'm a man like my dad.
If I sprint for the 8.53,
nobody thinks I am mad.

My trousers are hoist by a belt.
My conversation is dull.
I'm a first-class chap for my job.
My brains are kept down by my skull.

History too has a way
of being a terrible bore.
It repeats itself all the time.
It's supposed to follow some law.

Chaos we're told always threatens.
Anarchy's just kept at bay.
Roll over and turn off the light.
Thank God for another good day.

WHERE THE LAMPLIGHT FALLS

As a rule a poem will fit neatly onto an A4 typing sheet.
Short and to the point.
You can sum it up at a glance, a bit like a painting
or absorb it slowly like a cognac after dinner.
It enriches your life.
It is the perfect friend who never fails to amuse.

A poem always contains exactly the right number of words.
The concentration is amazing.
How did he do it?
You'd think it would be hermetic; but, no,
the result is accessible even to a reader
without much knowledge of 20th century poetry, its genres,
    its tendencies.

Other poems spill out over the page.
Formless, frameless.
They even resist the description, poem.
Will they find their place in world literature?
What do they say about the state of mind of the writer?
We will not talk about these poems now.
We will confine ourselves to the known, the familiar,
    the assimilable.

from

How to Get the Most
Out of Your Jet Lag

(2001)

FEET

This month's ill part of me will be my feet.
I distress myself looking at them.
How shiny they are, the skin could be Chinese paper,
surfaces like moon plateaux.

My feet are growing old faster than the rest of me –
though running on ahead would be an imprecise
    description.
Rather they stumble forward on their own momentum,
like a great power past its prime.

Crusty they are too, with fissures.
Less biology than geology.
Unsafe for walking on, a foot fetishist's worst case scenario.

I visit chiropodists all over town.
Each has a different version of what I should do.
They look at my two tombstones, mentally wringing their
    hands.
Mentally I watch them mentally wringing their hands.

Perhaps I'll need socks of elastic all my life.
Don't worry, they say. Flesh-coloured, they're almost
    invisible, they'll soon become part of you.

Various preparations may be applied, three times a day.
Don't expect a miracle however; you have unusually dry
    feet.

Others tell me the only solution may be surgery.
How everyone has it these days.

How you don't even need to overnight in hospital.
How with lasers it leaves no scar.

How I can get a replacement with feet of clay.

Next month I will celebrate my teeth.

HOLLAND'S GLORY

Supposing turnips not tulips were the national symbol.
There would be bull and bear markets in this root vegetable.
On the stock exchange they are traded in instead of bonds.

Eat them at your peril.
They'll have you locked up
or punished by whipping!

Fanciers are given time on national TV,
after the news, before the weather report.
Turnip arrangement is taught in first grade.

Young girls blush when their sweetheart suddenly shows up
    at their door, his arms full of the big round beauties.

Oh! harvest of a thousand breeds.
There are turnips for lovers,
others are suitable for birthdays or family occasions.
Are you taking your last leave of a loved one? Say it with
    turnips.

We praise them for their roundness,
for their vast size and luminosity,
for their freedom from knobs,
for their simplicity of form like the Buddha sunk in no
    mind at all.
Cattle are chased away from them with electric prods.

Like lanterns they illuminate the rain-soaked fields of
    Autumn.

And delegations come from China for the latest tips of
    their cultivation.

Oh secret of a lowlands destiny.
Benevolence, solemnity, stillness – human qualities
    compared to those of the turnip.
In the dreamless underground sleep of the turnip new
    worlds ripen slowly.
And new phrases are coined: 'Sow your turnips on time,
    your harvest is wisdom.'
'A good man, or woman is worth his/her weight in
    turnips'.
Or: 'Gold may vanish, but a turnip is for ever'.

Centuries of solitude, dedication and ingenuity
went into inventing that miracle, half nature, all artifice:

The black turnip.

RIDING HOME FROM BRIGHTON BEACH

for Lori

First we get drunk.
Then some mini-blinis.
The vodka (in a carafe!) was great.
It's June but deathly cold, fog wraps round the sea.
All seas are the same in the fog,
could be the Black Sea, say at Odessa.
Wraiths of Tchekovian silhouettes lining the boardwalk,
    old men barneying with each other.

I am grumpy
though the vodka cheers for a moment,
lifting the fringe of a curtain of an amazing world where
    nowhere is everywhere, where New York is Odessa,
where nostalgia is not even on film.
We are the film.

But this is a country for old men
and I feel old
in this cold.

Then we ride home to Greenpoint.
Back to Brooklyn, you say.
But we're in Brooklyn anyway, I say!
Brighton Beach is in Brooklyn.
First, you say, we have to go to Manhattan, to Sixth Avenue
    and catch the L train back to Brooklyn.
It's as though we were trying to sew Brooklyn and
    Manhattan together.

Back and forth.
Back and forth.

I am grumpy.
Of all the tall tales of the subway this is the longest.
You weren't talking to me, you say.
Darling, I was talking to you;
I was talking to you from a distance with my back turned.

Didn't you hear me muttering,
like the little waves along the shore,
nibbling away at the hard flat sand?

Soon there'll be not just half a subway car between us,
but an ocean or a sky.
But that shouldn't take much longer than a ride from
    Brighton Beach to Greenpoint! I say.
Maybe it'll only cost one subway token!
You get mad at me.

Oh don't get mad! oh come next flight!
We'll stitch New York and Europe together.
Making one big garment of our lives.

And we'll dine at home.
I'll make you shrimp and yoghurt soup.
Yes, and we'll drink Russian vodka
and never go out-of-doors again.
We'll wrap ourselves up in a big blanket
stitched out of all the cities of the world
and settle down.

HOW TO GET THE MOST OUT OF YOUR JET LAG

If you must fly, take a plane.
Try flying backwards.
Count time backward.
Lean forward to go forward.
Count your blessings before they're hatched.
Count yourself happy.
If you can't control yourself go all the way.
If you can't help being stupid, stand tall and proud.
If you land in jail return to New York.
Don't sleep before you're spoken to.
Catch up on lost sheep.
The sheep of the desert is a camel.
Passengers flying through the eye of a needle are only
    permitted to carry hand luggage.
The elephant of the skies is a Jumbo jet.
Give up smoking – set fire to a camel.
To fly safely is better than to arrive.

PESSOA PALIMPSEST

i

Today I feel totally confused, like someone who has
    forgotten everything he knew.
I'm a complete failure.
Not a dramatic one, just unimportant.
Instead of the philosopher's barrel, it's the dustbin of
    history for me.
I can't remember ever having done anything memorable
    in my life; perhaps it was all nothing.
I was taught plenty of things; no one can say I haven't had
    a good education; my knowledge might be called
    encyclopaedic; I threw it all away.
It wouldn't have done me any good anyway since I don't
    know who I am.

At this moment
thousands of people in this city
are fantasizing different lives for themselves – that they
    suddenly become rich and famous,
or have a legendary love affair
punctuated with anguish and heaped with joys.
None of them will be remembered either.

Maybe people will talk about them in their local bar for
    a while and then, like a candle,
those memories too will flicker and dwindle or be
    snuffed out.

Why should I be any different, just because my opinion
    of myself was mountainous?

ii

No. To be truthful I was overcompensating.
I have major doubts about myself.
I look in the mirror and see
something that tells me as much as my passport photo.

To say I look inscrutable would be making me sound
    mysterious.
I am not mysterious.
There's nothing there, hardly a shadow.
What I see is *nada, niks, niente*.

Mirror mortality on the wall,
all you tell me is I exist.
Yeah! I definitely exist.
I experience this fact as disappointing.
There's nothing there I can relate to,
any more than some family portrait by an unknown artist.

iii

I could be a distant ancestor of myself, painted by some
    useless minor artist.
The kind of artist who when told to paint, perhaps you
    have talent, went off and did it,
to keep himself out of mischief, to give himself something
    to do.
And when a few weeks later they came to his studio and
    viewed the results and pleaded with him to stop, he
    didn't listen.
He'd gotten into the knack, into the way of it. He started
    after breakfast.

He simply went on; he'd built up momentum doing these
    kitsch objects. It had become a habit, a way of life.

I tried to present myself as terribly clever.
But what I could have made of myself I didn't make.
I put on all kinds of poses:
the ultimate dandy, the bleeding Christ, the great lover, the
    intrepid traveller, the massive intellectual.
No one was fooled.
They knew better than I did who I was,
nor did they tire of telling me.
Preferably behind my back.

(Did I hear you correctly?)

Who am I to say they were wrong?

Once I put on a mask;
it became my face.

     iv

Everything is smoke.
If I don't regret anything it's because I'm stupid.
I might have been Edith Peron or Eva Pilaff.
Je ne regrette rien!
Stupid!

     v

I could have been Shakespeare. At least in my photos I look
    like Shakespeare, bald, enigmatic, non-committal.
I am a hundred different people and no one in particular.

I sit in a café and make normal conversation,
no-one's conversation is more ordinary than mine,
but I'm sympathetic, lively, I actually listen to other people,
    I'm well-liked in my local bar.

Everyone enjoys my jokes; I'm not a bad fellow,
even though I don't exist, am split and mad;
a rat scurrying down a dark corner,
no mind of my own.

Listen friends, I feel dreadful this morning.
I look at myself in the mirror. I am worse than a ghost.
When I walk down the street I feel like the last cowboy
after all the cowboys have been swallowed up by the movies,
a real cowboy, but in a world of fish stands and coffee shops,
where being a cowboy just means you're off your head.
I am that cowboy. I lost my horse in Lonesome Ranch.
Her name was Clementine, she ate Michaelmas daisies.
She had a sense of humour and irony as well.
Nobody feels irony as well as a cowboy's horse,
after the last saloon has been boarded up and the cowboy
    was born in Surrey.
Why worry? –
I was born in Surrey.
Did I say Surrey?
I said sorry.
Sorry, I was born in Sorry.

vi

Sorry if I made you cry
JOHN LENNON

Sorry if I'm bothering you.
Sorry if I'm in your way.
Sorry that I interrupted.
Sorry that I came to stay.

Sorry if I don't look sorry.
Sorry but I really tried.
Sorry I outstayed my welcome.
Sorry I broke down and cried.

Sorry I always missed the point.
Sorry if I changed my mind.
Sorry I didn't understand.
Sorry I wasted your precious time.

Sorry I didn't pay back that loan.
Sorry that I used your phone.
Sorry I messed your busy schedule.
I had no schedule of my own.
I couldn't stand to be alone.

Sorry that I bought that ground
for a burial in style
in an overpriced monument – you know,
one of those pointed ones along the Nile.

That way I'll go down in history
and have my cut of the cake of fame.
Though I was a frightful bore,
at least you won't forget my name.

vii

Stopping and Standing Still Song

It is as if
I'd spent my whole life
in the dentist's waiting room

and death was the dentist

and as if
life was a train
I'd slept in past the stop

and as if

there's light at the end of the tunnel
but no light in between

Oh life's too short
to be so long
        sometimes.

Oh life's too short
to be so long
        sometimes.

HOLY MACKEREL

The mackerel wears a mackintosh
to keep him dry at sea:
blue, black and silver, rather punk
and trendy as can be.
But still he lands up on my plate
where he glares reproachfully.
Should I feel bad this lovely fish
Was swallowed up by me?

RENOUNCING POETRY

I'm gonna get off that poetry train
before it leaves the tracks
or careens off down a side line,
and never comes back.

    With my life on board.

Gonna give up writing poems,
Find something sane to do
to occupy my time.
Could be something useful too.

Whoever heard such a thing?
Poetry saved no lives.
Didn't glue the social fabric.
No. Poets just lived in dives,

Got pissed as two-humped camels,
talked the whole night long,
arguing their heads off,
proving everybody wrong,

    excepting for themselves.

No, I'm gonna get up and go,
see some daylight hours,
pay the next gas instalment.
Never mind the soul!

What sort of a person would do that –
starving in a gutter
like someone off his head?
You'd have to be a nutter

to sit up through the night,
trying to make things rhyme.
There's nothing worse than iambic verse
when you ain't got a dime.

Gonna give up this addiction
before it gives up on me.
Gonna live like people used to
back in 1943:

Dad brought home the bacon.
Ma put it on the boil.
Bombs were raining all around.
Fruit of honest toil.

Soon the war will be over.
Give peace a chance.
Don't let the poets spoil it
with their drunken Maenad dance.

I'm gonna get off that poetry train
before it leaves the tracks
or careens off down a side line,
and never comes back.

    With my life on board.

Or I'll lie around a little
till my beard starts growing long,
waste a mammoth heap of time
glooming about my wasted life,

wake up from my dumb despair,
all the things I've been doing wrong,
write a brand new poem,
call it: 'Resurrection Song'.

CHICKEN WITH MADNESS

What do they say about the poets?
Never heard of us.
Didn't know we still existed.
Do we, in fact?
Exist.
Are we real? That's the big question!

This is what they say about us:
We're so outside of everything.
We're so marginal we can't be taken seriously.
We're so arrogant we think we're doing something epoch-
    shaking.
We fool ourselves we can change history writing poems.
Nobody buys our books except in jumble sales.
What we write is incomprehensible,
obscure,
unreadable,
boring,
long-winded,
self-indulgent.
Decadent.

We make a fetish of decadence.
We think of sex the whole time.
We don't go to bed at normal hours.
Our brains are full of cobwebs.
We are walking examples of the harm done by masturbation.
We can't write without the aid of artificial stimuli – drugs
    or alcohol.

We are totally lacking in self-discipline.
We represent a persistent and endemic failure of the will,
    typical of our time.

We are incapable of any great works.
The forms of poetry are finished.
Nothing awaits us but insanity and an early grave.

We fritter away our talent.
We just live for kicks.
We don't do any useful work.
We are burnt-out cases.
We don't contribute anything to the community.
We are always out of money.
We make a cult of idleness.
We are emotionally immature.

We have a Peter Pan complex.
We have a Hamlet complex.
We have a Faust complex.
We have an Electra complex.
We have a Medea complex.
We have a Tristan complex.
We have an Antigone complex.
We have a Cinderella complex.
We have a Don Juan complex.

We have a vitamin B complex.

We have the arrogance without the genius.
We are crippled by a nostalgia for childhood.

We are incapable of action.
We don't take part in real life.
We are lifestyle anarchists.
We tell the youth there is no future.
There is no future, youth!
We rot the moral fibre of the nation.
We prophesy doom.
We indulge in despair.
We stir up trouble just for the sake of it.
We manipulate the language. Yes, folks, that's what!
    We manipulate the language!

(You get a picture of the language before the poets came
    along.
It was a given, a thing without history.
It was a pure, pristine, abstract, virgin thing.
Smiling, ready for use, always available, serviceable –
with spare parts in case anything goes wrong,
and a built-in obsolescence factor.
Like the perfect call-girl in a quiet modern flat in a discreet
    suburb
with pink telephone and shrimp-pink curtains –
marvellous how language is almost entirely a decor item
    nowadays! –
and perfumed shower curtains and playing with her vibrator,
so she is warmed up and ready for you,
available for a small fee, even to the common man,
especially to the common man – the English language.
It would have to be English: what other language is there
('This royal throne of kings, this sceptred isle . . . '),
current everywhere like a Master credit card?

And then we came along, the poets, with our loud ways
and our dirty, underhand, sneaky, silent ways
and our pure, mad, idealistic, iconoclastic, quixotic mysticism.
And our silly jokes.
Cutting up sentences to pieces and putting them back in
    the wrong order,
pouring it all into the retorts in our secret language
    laboratories,
recreating it right from scratch in the underground fallout
    shelters of our deranged brains,
making it impossible for anyone to have just a normal
    conversation over a cup of tea ever again!).

We have no respect for tradition.
We are incapable of anything new.
We only know how to destroy.
A good old-fashioned war, that would do us good.
We are work-shy pacifists.
We are a dying breed.
We betray all the signs of obsolescence.
We are being replaced by word-processors and word-
    professors.
We don't exist any more.
I don't exist.
I am no longer myself.
This is not me talking to you.
This is Faust at midnight talking to you.
How can he prove he is a poet?
How can he prove he is not kidding himself?
He is the victim of the delusion that he is a poet.
A self-induced delusion.

Probably I disappeared through a black hole in my own
     mind.
All my life I have been digging that black hole.
All my life I have been trying to find myself.
Digging a black hole trying to find myself!
Maybe I am mad.
I need a psychiatrist.
No psychiatrist would take me on.
I persist in my sickness.
I have wasted my life!

Writing poetry isn't a job.
It's an excuse. A hobby. An alibi. A permanent vacation.
The only good poet is a dead poet.

They accuse us of stealing the moon.
Of having no cake and eating it.
Of talking a lot of nonsense in tongues.

Plato said it all:
never trust a poet.
We say we are obsessed with truth – we don't know what
     truth is.
Nobody knows who we are, least of all ourselves.
We have so many masks we never show our real face.
A cheap tranced-out smile, that's what we show the world.
We walk around exalted, ecstatic, half-crazed, delirious,
     talking to ourselves out loud, dancing, chanting.
It's true, we do!
We totter endlessly on the brink of a nervous breakdown.
We experiment with our brains.
We play chicken with madness.

We are schizophrenics and psychotics.
There is a 76% rate of suicides among us.
We are erotomaniacs and occultists.
We dabble in the occult and the black arts.
We are melancholics, manic depressives, megalomaniacs.
We are sadists. We are masochists. We are sado-masochists
and maso-sadochists.
We are spoilt middle-class brats.
We are not as interesting as we think we are.
We are over-intellectual decadent wankers.
We suffer from mystical delusions.
We are hopelessly out of touch with reality.
We have odd ideas about God.
(I am like a walking nightmare   haunted   haunted!)
We are ingenious liars. We are born poseurs. We are perverts.
We give a new dimension to the word 'pervert'.

Our trances are self-induced.
We are exhibitionists, narcissists, catatonics.
The whole psychiatric laundry list applies.

Poètes maudits   poètes maudits   poètes maudits!
Let's translate it for once. See how it sounds.
Poeti dannati?
Gedoemde dichters?
Damned poets!

Who says we're damned?
And what is hell?

MY HONEYMOON WITH MYSELF

Under the stars of Naples,
alone at last!
In the hotel I booked the queen-sized matrimonial suite.

Friends and family gave me a great send-off.
My aged mother, tears in her eyes, waving goodbye:

'I'm glad to see you finally settled.
You weren't exactly the easiest person to live with.'

'Great, mother,' I say, 'finally I've found someone you
        really approve.'

Yet after all the excitement I don't know what to think.
Is it love that I feel?
or did I just talk myself into it?
Won't I get bored?

And, indeed, next morning at breakfast in the hotel dining
        room
the atmosphere is a little subdued.

Everybody smiles as they look at me.
What must they be thinking?

Suddenly I'm a stranger, even to myself.

I look at myself, my downcast eyes.
Will conversation always be this hard?

And I wonder:
did I make the right choice?
Will I make myself happy?

Should I have spent more time surveying the field?

But as the mist lifts from the sea,
like a curtain opening on distant islands,
perhaps there is hope.

A stroll along the cliffs might cheer my spirits.

Still the nagging doubt:
I wasn't quite sure if I was a virgin.

from

The Glittering Sea

(2006)

QUESTIONS TO ASK WHEN IT'S LOVE
AT FIRST SIGHT

How old are you?
Do you already have a friend?
What work do you do,
or are you still studying?
Are you a vegetarian or do you eat meat too?
Oh! fish. One of those vegetarians.
I forgot what I wanted to say to you.
I forget what we were talking about anyway.
Do you mind if I touch you here?
What planet do you come from?

I LIKE MY HERON

Dissonant dinosaur of a bird,
claws gingerly stepping along
the corrugated roof of the city farm
he's made his home.

(So he can steal the rabbits' breakfast?)

Closest bird to prehistory,
knobbly knees and straight-out flight,
his shriek cuts the sky like a piece of chalk,
saying:

'So many fish I've had,
I am what I eat.
I can swim the sky.'

Now standing erect,
tall and bony,
head turned 180 degrees,

looks like some non-violent philosopher,
if you're not a fish.

Meanwhile a 20-yard long, 12-wheeled articulated
    tyrannosaurus
has just turned the corner
heading towards the building site opposite,
riding the wrong way down our one-way evolutionary
    street.

Cars get the hell out of here!
Dogs scram!
No more parking
or barking!

The Amsterdam heron,
symbol of restraint in meditation
rules my roost.
That's my bird!

BICYCLE ON ICE

Got home late
calvados in the tapas bar
was to blame

it was drizzling ice
a cold mist

rose from the freezing waters
of the Brouwersgracht

a gleaming skin of skid
on hump-backed bridges

I saw
a young woman on her bike

swivel in a dazzling unplanned
figure of eight

from vertical
to horizontal

some rode to rescue her
not a wise move so it proved

bikes spreadeagled on a street of glass
like a heap of the slain

others wavering in pure good will
did their best just standing still

call me deserter if you like
I crawled back on hands and knees

dragging bike
like a stubborn dog

clung to parapet with one hand
bike with other

almost wrapped around myself
but how to move when move meant slide

trying to push myself and bike
at the same time forward

alcohol was my wheels
trepidation did the splits

who knows how I made it home
slept like a frozen doorstep

bike steaming in its shed
old nag stabled at last

DANCING WITH AN OCTOPUS

for Marlo Broekmans

Fantastic organizer,
genius networker,
arms
everywhere at once.

      Beauty –
      and brains!

and that enduring sadness of
insatiable sea things.

How not to feel
love at first fright?
How not to fall for him?
      If feeling is believing,
      how not be taken in?

And should you slip into the ocean,
and should he slide all arms around you,
then let him lead your dance
across the ocean floor
      in one long quickstep glide;
or follow him in deepest tango swoon
down avenues of seaweed fronds
– watch out, he may elide
your life in one cold amorous embrace
and lead you to his very private place
where nothing makes much difference any more.

And please don't dare
to look him in his mournful eye –
lest he bewitch you with his stare;
his sorrow is an endless maw
it would take more than you to fill.

And don't forget,
ask him politely when the music stops
(serenade of uncurling shrimps and hurtling crabs,
where flat things flap along
to sea-bass undertones)
      if he will kindly let you up,
      unsquelch his squelchers just a mo:

'Excuse, Sir Octopus,
before I finally go down
to share with you the unthinkable delights
of your château where starfish wink
and sea anemones bejewel –
      such darling little blobs –
          that turquoise grotto, your peculiar home,
I have to go
      and get my scarf and shoulder-bag – you know,
my woman's things –
can you imagine, dear,
I must have left them on those rocks up there
      where all is sunlight and translucent air
so different from your milieu.'

And back on shore –
one shout flung like a pebble at all that green –

'Dear Octopus I had to go –
d'you think you'll manage on your own?
I hope you'll understand,
I'm not quite sure we'd be compatible.
I'm more a surface girl.'

O polpo mio, adorato,
sei stato così garbato.
Ma non posso immaginare
di poter vivere felice in fondo al mare.
Altra scelta non ho io
che dirti tristemente addio.

And shivering on the bright sand, thank your stars
you did not join his store of bones.

THE AMSTERDAM ZOO AS A WORK
OF CONCEPTUAL ART

In its apparent obsession with enclosed spaces,
this huge installation occupying a number of acres of
    good building land
reminds me of no-one so much

as the Russian-born installation artist, Ilya Kabakov,
who uses paranoia as an aesthetic device.
We cannot escape the idea that we too may be 'shut in'

in more ways than we know
and there is the frightening suggestion that the animals
    might take over.
It is hardly a new observation that the great apes resemble
    us,

still we may ask why the artist has included them here.
Are they to remind us of our *condition bête*
or to teach us to know our place?

Particularly ingenious with its post-modern, layered
    character
is a compound containing 'camels', several long-beaked
    'birds'
and what I can only describe as a designer animal, a creature
    resembling an ox,
but executed in an extraordinary russet brown with
    provocatively straight horns.

Everywhere there are barriers
preventing the viewers from interacting with the object
    viewed.
One may not, should one wish, embrace a 'snake',

making this exhibit rather disappointing in terms of viewer
    participation.
True, these are found objects, but I don't think Duchamp
    would have applauded.
Somewhere the whole work lacks an intellectual dimension.

Interesting however is the inclusion of an array of 'children' –
they are everywhere, vivid, swarming,
engaged in typical childish activities, such as eating 'ice
    cream'.

Personally I think a minimalist approach would have
    worked as well,
with just a few, less exotic creatures – some 'cats',
a 'rabbit' or two, a tame 'dog' –
but with infinite repetitions and subtle gradations.

Some invented animals too, à la Calvino, would have made
    the work less literal,
though I did enjoy certain bizarre juxtapositions –
a paddock of miniature 'deer' for instance, the size of large
    rats,

next door to a giant woolly 'dromedary',
and a cage of 'humming birds' within smelling distance
    of an 'Indian rhinoceros'.
The artist's ambition is to say the least encyclopaedic.

97

Absent however is any attempt at ordering this chaos.
And isn't the fixation with cage constructions a bit over
    the top?
Wouldn't the 'penguins', left free, develop their own order?
Or the 'lions' be somehow less predictable, on the loose?

Despite the post-modern touches, then, this is a primitive
    creator.
It's almost *art brut*, this wild exuberance.
There is so much of everything — it's so in-your-face.

We are unable to see the bestiary for the beasts.
Was the artist making an ironic comment on the
    impossibility of being God,
or did he just walk away from his project?

CENTRAL PARK VISTAS

i

I am sitting on a bench in Central Park.
February. The sun, pale horseman in a lukewarm sky.
The trees complaining they're naked.
As if looking through a window,
I watch the human *passeggiata*.

Each has his destiny –
but it's a layered, postmodern destiny,
perfectly tailored to our age of limited possibilities
where we negotiate our free moments like small change.

Everyone is heading somewhere, purposeful.
They have their game plans; their time slots are filled; their
    week is worked out.
It's ordinary life I'm witnessing – lucid, functional, proud,
    together, self-absorbed.

Here come the joggers and fast walkers –
a fellow with fat, almost hairless thighs, working his weight
    off.
Two fit young women pacing each other.
Then a biker full-tilt – wow! with turned-up handlebars,
    beating his arms across his chest! But it's realistic, he's
    not showing off!
He's exercising at once both thighs and pectorals; it looks
    like a stunt but it's deadly serious.
No-one could accuse him of not cramming his life with
    meaning,

or call his behaviour threatening and ludicrous.
His gestural language isn't a cry for help.
The babies playing in the sand look up as he speeds past,
    but are undismayed.

A woman sits peacefully down the bench from me, reading
    her Times, her skin blotchy and pale;
she could be recovering from a long illness.
Her vulnerable, simpering gaze does not mean she wants
    to strike up a conversation –
I smile but she doesn't smile back.
It could come from poor digestion – it's more a grimace
that illuminates her otherwise private face.
She is sitting here in the pre-spring sunlight to aid her
    convalescence,
not to talk to a stranger with nothing better to do.

Oh! roller-bladers, stately as old five-masters,
weaving their way around us like visiting angels,
cleaving an invisible furrow as if writing on air.

But I'm just watching them, a tourist, meaningless.
I'm the why on the wall, hunched like a question mark.
I am running from my responsibilities.
I am spending money foolishly.
I am far from home,
pursuing a chimera.
Mentally I don't have a home
(not even a mental home).
But that doesn't make me an existentialist –
it's just the same old muddle going round.

Home is where the heart is — but where, oh where is
    the heart?
Picking up the shards, no doubt, of some ludicrous love
    affair.

(Oh! love can't buy you money!)

I wonder what it feels like to be American.
Try as I may, I am not American.
It's a total non-starter of a project to want to be American.
Jean-Paul Sartre would make mincemeat of it.

What's the use, they will say, admiring other people's culture,
    when you've got a perfectly good one of your own?

I go through the motions; I'm always smiling.
I have social intercourse several times a week.
I participate in various sports. I am not in debt. My hand-
    shake is firm. I seem honest. I resemble myself.
My conversation is lucid; I entertain ideas.
I am a good listener. I give sound advice
when someone tells me of their difficult situation.
I have my own viewpoint — but a carefully qualified one,
    it contains self-irony.
My thoughts appear to be my own — they don't look like
    borrowed clothes, nor did I buy them off the peg.
I have never been institutionalised or deemed mad.
I was a sixties anti-hero, but made the right adjustments.
I am a professional translator.
I have several résumés; if you want I can show you one.

I'll tell you a secret – I'm a performance poet. Oh!
    glamorous and strange! –
good topic if I want to make an impression at a party.
But then they say, 'What are they like, your poems? What
    do they say?
Nothing? How can you fill up paper saying nothing?
    Think of the trees!'

There is something immoral, but also contemptible about
    having nothing to say and insisting on saying it.
I mean, not evil like a serial killer, just a low-grade
    perversion, like masturbation. Ah! there you have me –
Donald Gardner, translator, performance poet, serial wanker
    and ultimate tourist.

ii

Will I be spoken of?
Will I be remembered?

'He was a tourist; he didn't fully participate.
Life passed him by like one of those subway trains at 3 am,
honking, empty, far too fast, not stopping,
leaving you standing on the platform where only the
    muggers lurk, and all you want is to get back home
    and be in bed.

Even his goodness was somehow contingent.

Nervous-making, ill-at-ease, too plausible.
As if he was using you for an alibi. You didn't know where
    you stood with him.
You never knew if he was thinking something.

He was hard to love; he shrunk into himself.
And yet', they will say, 'it was his own fault;
somehow he conspired to make himself unlovable.
He was his own worst enemy – he didn't need others.'

iii

I embrace philosophers: but none of them explain my
    condition.
Embracing them is just another part of my tourism –
adopting ideas like a bus shelter late at night when the rain
    is falling and the buses have stopped running.
I embrace them; I embrace smoke.

Only sometimes in sex I exist.
there is no before or after; it feels transcendent –
never mind with whom.

iv

And yet at the first hint of Spring American possibilities
    fan out like birds breaking cover.
The afternoon's beautiful here in the park and, yes, the sun
    is a ghost, but it's still warm enough to sit outside.
Young couples are lapping each other up in broad daylight
    – without a steady girlfriend, I still get pleasure
    watching them.
Let no-one call me a voyeur!

Oh! landscaped park both beautiful and useful,
where even a tourist may relax a while,
alienated from himself and his surroundings, maybe even
    fallen through a glitch in history,

but still free to sit in the February sun, unobjectionable,
    just a figure in a scene,
where one can contemplate a life where future and past
    have some meaning,
where something more than absurdity is one's lot.

And then I see it – my epiphany!
The dog walker – amazing – clasping the lines of his
    charges like a unique assorted bouquet,
reining them in at the curb
as though offering them to the universe,
or perhaps to me.

Big glistening beauties, all on their mettle – Afghans,
    Borzois, a dwarf poodle, even a couple of mutts.
If this is the world, I'm part of it.
Make my day! Splendiferous! Life is holy! Yelp!

PARTS OF SPEECHLESSNESS

In these states of emergency
adjectives are inadequate to describe
the nouns that used to make such great labels
only they've stopped sticking to things.
They still try and do something useful –
even if it's only looking busy
while sitting around;

but the verbs
just refuse to be conjugated
and pronouns
prove suddenly interchangeable.

A persistent 'we' and 'them'
tries to assert itself.
Few are convinced.

The little prepositions
go seeking for cover.
'No-one', they say,
'appreciates any more
what a good job we do.'

Waving a flag
and waving goodbye
become for the time being
one and the same thing.

DUST SHEET

Like a pit of sacrifice,
this sudden amphitheatre
where light pours down like rain.

Like rabbits in a headlight blaze,
we're hypnotized by what we see
but do not yet believe.
Like little puppets in death's ham fist.

Like all those dreams where I forget my lines,
revealing what I always knew at heart –
and this is what breaks the heart –
how redundant we have always been
on any weighty scene
where governments and assassins tread the boards.

Like a group by Auguste Rodin,
a grey herd of citizens
is driven towards the camera,
yet petrified
in monumental freeze
by its Medusa lens.

Like a Christo artwork gone dreadfully wrong,
dust drapes the city,
stopping our pores
like a huge conspiracy.

THE GLITTERING SEA

I dreamed I fell from the highest building,
but that highest building was me.
For my work took me to the ninetieth floor
down by the glittering sea.

My sweetheart said, 'Don't go in today,
just snuggle up close to me.'
I said, 'Sweet, you're naughty to say such a darling thing,
but I'm saving for you and me.'

She said, 'Tell your boss you're sick or so,
we'll lie in a little bit more.'
But I sighed and slipped into my clothes
and out of our bedroom door.

She turned to the wall and closed her eyes
but didn't sleep in for long.
She woke to a blaze of TV news,
and remembered where I'd gone.

Oh! please, dear God, make me late for work
down by the glittering sea.
Let some minor incident slow my train
to those canyons down by the sea.

I dreamed I fell from the highest building,
but that highest building was me.
For my work took me to the ninetieth floor
by the glittering, glittering sea.

CROW CROW

Crow crow
in my mother's garden.
She feeds you all her stale bread.

Crow crow
plunging down from the neighbour's chimney,
leaving nothing for blackbird and robin.

Crow crow,
the thrushes will have a grand party
when you are on the wing.

Perched on your lookout post
or dipping crusts in the little pond.
Crafty old thing.

Portentous stare and weighty walk,
not all dark suits are criminals
but you wear black and look louche,

with grey tail feathers
as if that black were singed to ash.

You could be the taxman just dropping by
to advise me on outstanding payments.

Loan shark, undertaker, stand-up comic
masquerading as a bird.

Crow crow,
my mother fed you all she had,
her skinny arms
tossing leftovers of Waitrose's cardboard dinners.

Best readymade food in town
And nothing less will do
as you waddle across the lawn
the gardener shaved for you.

Crow crow,
one day she fed you a whole packet of puff-pastry,
muttering under her breath,
'one bird less won't do any harm'.

Crow crow,
did it swell and swell inside you?

One day you'll just fall out of the sky.
No wings then will help you fly.

And blackbird, robin and thrush will fly back in
and warble and crow and sing.

PIGEONS

Dear Mother,
the crows on your lawn

have been evicted
by the pigeons next-door –

mini-vultures,
reptiles on wings,

cold eyes
homing in on your home,

shitting on the bird-table
to stake their claim.

At the far end of your garden
if I walk after dark,

I trigger the neighbour's
halogen lamp,

a pool of light
on your lawn.

Things encroach
now you're gone.

The roots
of the copper beech

tilt at your
Edwardian foundations.

Gunge in my lungs
this lonesome June.

The doctor
suggests depression,

prescribes
a sledgehammer.

At ninety-four
you stopped growing old.

I'm catching up with you now.
Like some sad Everest,

will I make it
to the top,

or winded on those heights
end muffled in snow?

TRAIN DRAIN

This train got started at Leytonstone.
This train could hardly bear to leave Leyton,
only really got going at Stratford,
decided it wasn't worth it at Mile End,
opted for the category of non-achiever at Bethnal Green,
changed for the Metropolitan and Circle Lines at Liverpool
    Street,
lost all grip on reality at the Bank.
This train took leave of its senses at Saint Paul's.

> *This train has drained the sweetness out of life, including the
>   nostalgia for sweetness.*
> *This train stole love from me and gave me a career with
>   prospects,*
> *stole my ability to feel love and compensated me with money.*
> *This train made sex into a commodity item.*
> *This train carries in its bowels the memories of the beautiful
>   trains:*
> *Train Bleu, Trans Siberian, the Orient and Rome expresses,
>   the Cairo-Luxor train rushing with joy down the blue,
>   yellow, green valley of the Nile where white egrets flew
>   between palms.*
> *It would like to be these trains, but oh! no, this train is destined
>   to convey commuters,*
> *silence coagulating between passengers,*
> *poker-faced sadnesses behind newspapers.*

This train is adept at making major pronouncements
    between stations,
got off and walked round the platform at Chancery Lane,
enjoyed a mid-life crisis at Holborn,
rode again from the dead at Tottenham Court Road.
At Oxford Circus stopped for water,
mumbled in its beard at Bond Street.

That's right, blame it on the train,
stopping between all stations.
That life's not what it used to be.
That you didn't turn things as you'd have liked them,
got stuck in obsolete tunnels, never exited to light.
That your relationships got bogged down in a condition like
    lumpy porridge.

This train killed God, and replaced him with cybernetics.
Witnessed the slow dissipation of old friendships.
This train produced a new, annotated version of the
    lamentations of Jeremiah.
Where light became a legendary thing,
and colour an unheard-of dimension.

This train rolled over and wanted its tummy tickled at
    Marble Arch,
had a bout of asthma at Lancaster Gate,
ululated at Queensway,
ejaculated at Notting Hill Gate.
This train excavated itself at Holland Park.

This train eradicated itself at Shepherds Bush,
extinguished itself at White City,
distinguished itself at East Acton,
but not in any way that was intended.

It never knew what was intended.
It was the fault of the train that you became derailed.
That you can't have your life over again.
That no ticket refund is possible.
You made your journey and you must pay for it.

This train exterminates at North Acton.
This train attempted euthanasia on itself at West Acton.
This train terminates at Ealing Broadway.

Step out at Ealing Broadway,
dazzled by the steel-grey daylight.
Somewhere I've never been before.
Maybe not such a bad place after all.
Products in serried ranks in all the supermarkets.
A racially mixed population.
Gaps of sky between the housing estates.
A thousand new impressions.
Ealing for ever!

from
The Wolf Inside
(2014)

THE WOLF INSIDE

downstairs five to seven
caught the weather forecast

like a bad cold
could have looked outside instead

radio blares out
as I make my tea

still dark at seven
even darker than yesterday

for some reason
time seems to be going backward

make a cuppa but first
open back door and slam straight shut

but the wolf got in anyway
a raging blast

scouring the larder
howling around the kitchen

furiously licking
the four walls

clean like an empty jam jar
then out once more

but I caught his tail
as I slammed the door

hungry wind
hungry wolf

stinking tail
of a cold wet wolf

rotten way
to start the day

READING THE POET AS HIS POETRY

decided to take a look
at the poet not the poetry

to read the poet
as his poetry

gave him three marks out of ten
for lifestyle

hardly an innovator
though he made a great nuisance of himself

raided the larder at 1 am
for supplies of marmite-flavoured twiglets

committed mixed metaphor
in relationships

mistook people for each other
kissed his enemies

did he influence
future generations

did he pass on the message
of the great tradition

adding his own thumbprint
to magnificence

no he came down
late for breakfast

forgot to return
borrowed money

on his bicycle
knocked down old ladies with shopping carts

his poetry was marvellous
passed him

like an Aston Martin
on the motorway

leaving him standing
no apparent connection

KEPT ALIVE BY MODERN MEDICINE

The idea of explaining oneself to the young,
telling them how much better things were when we
    were young.
How we revelled in our youth.

How we could teach the young to be young.
Sketch out a few dance steps to show them what we mean,
what it was to be young in the nineteen sixties.

Terrific!
How being young
will never be the same again.
How we drank youth to the full,
never wasting a moment.
Or if we did, we wasted it to the full,
blind, ruinously.

Did we blow it or swing it?
Same difference.

Look folks, we blew it completely,
the grand gesture.
Not like you lot, barely out of college
saving for your retirement.

How we're not shy to say it
now we're old fogeys.
Fogeys of freedom,
no obvious usefulness.
After us not the deluge
but a cold douche.

MOONRISE

On the far side of the Westerdok
they're building new flats
twelve storeys in Amsterdam

a crane slices the evening sky
two big lamps with the firm's name
on the crossbar

hanging like moons
in the November dusk
while the real moon

looks like a bad-tempered pinched little baby
dandled upwards
by the crossbar

as if ushered
sky-high
by real estate developers

later at 4 am
a steel-blue light wakes us
and we peer from our bedroom window

on the far side of the house
from its absolute height
the same moon

is gazing down
on our sleep-
drenched state

as if dangling
by a thread
from eternity

UNDER THE WEATHER

I am standing with my love
on Battersea Bridge
in the first heat wave of summer.

Along the Embankment the river of cars is unbroken
but the Thames, lowest water on record,
has the look of a pool being drained

and the sky, pale colour of urine,
is furrowed with flight paths
like a forehead frowning with age.

Helicopters,
giant blades
harvest the late-afternoon haze.

One I saw in mid air
hovering motionless
in a furious standoff with Battersea Power Station.

It's as if a huge membrane,
transparent as a featherlite condom,
has been stretched

between us and the sky,
a dome of millennial malevolence
between us and infinity.

Or else the sky really is the limit,
a plangent lid
under which we seethe,

no longer an ever-receding cerulean blue
promising infinity,
but an echo chamber

where our words are thrown back at us,
our broken promises and good intentions,
and hell is hearing ourselves speak.

On this evening on Battersea Bridge
the gentlest emotion
is a wistful sadness

but the kiss you plant on my cheek
is light as a butterfly
riding on a blade,

readying itself for take-off.
Maybe it doesn't change anything,
but all attempts are welcome.

MORNING SHIFT

8 am Starbucks
Astor Place

the first crop
of office workers shows up

clipped speech at the counter
as they order

their coffee and Danish
I'm up there with the best of them

but when I turn round
I glimpse the street people

sliding from the benches
where they may sleep in the small hours

by leave of the management
in bitter frost

one after another
a larval stir

of old stiff overcoats
shuffling outside

at the signal of the first comers
through the swing doors

the whole event
a conversation-stopper

but played out
in absolute silence

and taking
almost no time at all

leaving us to enjoy
the heady tang of Jamaican

Blue Mountain coffee
more or less undisturbed

IN THE ALDER THICKET

Choreography of kingcups
splayed out
as if flung by a hand
across the strip of meadow by the pool
     where the ducks wait
their turn
       digging deep in their feathers
          for ticks

and further on, a coot, white-billed, long-legged,
stalking demurely to the pool,
like a Victorian lady with girded drawers.

Two trains cross
and a runner speeds by.

I'm lost to the world; no,
it's more that, neither sleeping nor waking,
I become the world, feel its slow turn.

(A couple go past,
a woman with headdress
and her husband scolding her.
The ducks make their escape; she
goes off and sits on a bench, head bowed.)

In the first touch of summer you surmise its end –
dusty August, late afternoon,
a heat haze dumbfounds the blue,

while thunder peals along the horizon,
like a set of bowling balls,
or a plane circling off course
lost to all runways.

Parched grass.
This is my secret garden
where I disappear for an afternoon,
yet even here
I feel the city drawing near.
Amsterdam
spread out behind me like a carpet,
threadbare, the pattern faded, frayed at the edges.

Silence hemmed in by sounds.
Voices of passers-by
distant as voices in a dream.
A plane homing in low to Schiphol airport.

And then there is the sound of silence,
that even the shrill piping of insects
or the moorhen's splash as it somersaults,
hardly disturbs.

IN THE VONDELPARK

In the afternoon light
the pond in the Vondelpark
is glassy and still
as if the August sun
had covered it with a veil of ice.

A willow leans an arm
towards the water,
fishing
for something it dropped there yesterday,

while a flotilla of ducks
zips open the surface,

plying back and forth
like notes of music on a bar.

THE UNWELCOME DINNER

It was intended to have been a delicious dinner invitation.
Posh, in a hotel, in The Hague,
with alumni from my old university.
Five courses, two glasses of wine free, seventy-five euros.
I could meet some people I would never normally see!
Book well in advance, said the letter,
to avoid disappointment.
Cancel with two days' notice or we'll have to charge you.

Otherwise you'll have to pay.
I turned it over night and day.
I'd booked – but was my heart really in it, this classy binge?
Was it really me?

At the last moment
I didn't go.
Paid for not going.
Paid for no dinner.

It was worth the price.

IN THE GARFAGNANA

Summer had already marched a long way into Autumn
when we drove into the hills.
At a height of 1500 metres
with the road surging upward into San Pellegrino
through the swirling mist,
it seemed
we had reached the end of the known world.
A blind view and sheer curves on the road down
but, more than in the mist,
we were lost in each other.

ANGELA WILL SEE TO MY CORRESPONDENCE

When I'm dead
I won't need to meet any deadlines.
When my time has come
they'll stretch me out in bed,

at least until the doctor's been,
who, when I lived,
always said the same

(after a quick glance at my tongue
and reaching distractedly for my pulse):

'You're well enough to go to work.'

And will I arise and go now
(the force of habit can be strong)
to my desk in that fierce-lit office block,
with a bleak smile –
'I decided to come in after all!'

And the rest of the staff on the eleventh floor
are standing in clusters round the coffee automat,
nudging each other:

'Are you sure you feel all right?
Oughtn't you to have stayed at home?
Don't worry,
Angela will see to your backlog.'

And to each other:
'I recognise the suit,
but doesn't his face
look a little bit strained?
Perhaps it's just stress.'

'It *is* him though, isn't it?'

When I'm dead
Angela will attend to my outstanding correspondence
that seemed so urgent when alive.

See me in my coffin
with a cheerful grin,
flashing my teeth
before the final curtain.

No more trips to the dentist either.
My teeth are done,
their race is run.
Tricked by the embalmer's art,
they all came in more or less even in the end
as they never did when I was vertical.

FEAR OF WRITING

i

The pollution of the white page
the lewdness

exposing myself to the world
best keep it to myself

the terror
of error

doing battle with emptiness
riding a lance at

my own impotence
a fulltime Don Quixote

while others
no thanks to me

keep the world
rolling on.

ii

When I lift my pen
the hair rises on my head

if I were shaggy like a wolf
it would rise along my spine

I feel the hair
rising along my spine

having nothing to say
I set down words

if I did not
I would howl

I am a wolf
and the fear of a wolf

a bundle of fear without fur
an ancient scary creature

my voice echoes
in the primal forest

deeply troubled by the fear of dying
while I write I know I live.

THE NEW WOLF

Beasts of prey such as the wolf and the lynx
will soon be returning to Holland. The ecologist
Wouter Helmer will be only too delighted to see
these creatures return. Helmer was recently
awarded the Edgar Doncker Prize, with a sum
of 150,000 euros, for his project, 'Missing Lynx'.

DE VOLKSKRANT, 14 June 2008

They are bringing back the wolves.
Bears and lynx, the prehistoric horse
and above all the wolves.

But this is a new wolf with green credentials,
shot with digital cameras instead of guns.

Recently they have been sighted foraging in dustbins
near the local primary school, or in the park
madly chasing their tail or retrieving a stick.

Their attempts to form packs break down in silliness
as they sniff each other, bumper to bumper.
And at night they loll by the living-room radiator,
or sleep in the cat's basket, with the cat.

Only remember
when you let him out last thing,
the risk remains
he may revert to type

and come thundering back in, jaws blazing,
breaking the door down and
wrecking your hastily cobbled philosophies.

The cat creeps dolefully towards those jaws
and your children, your babies – oh! your babies! –
have been carried off to whatever forests still remain.

ON A PHOTOGRAPH OF MYSELF, AGED TWO

I am all there
all my hair
thick blonde curls
concentrating fiercely on a box of alphabet blocks.
In the photo I look
definitely unimpressed –
twenty-six letters,
that's not much of an alphabet!

My sister's in the photo too,
keeping an eye on me to see I don't make a mess,
but she's been messing with my toy battleship.
Better watch it, big sister, I'm thinking.
But I'd better watch it myself – she's bigger than me.
Older, bigger, spoiling for a fight,
she'll see I don't get into mischief.

Nearly seventy years on, I catch myself
in the same pose.
Hands on hips, same vexed look.
I'm staring at my grandchildren as they move around
    the living-room floor,
crawling and playing,
but my mind is elsewhere.
In company, but lost.

All that change,
yet I'm still the same.

Only today
I might be hard put to it
to get into mischief.

DEATH DOES TENNIS

Now the last set begins, the deciding rallies.
Mr Death, not previously known for his prowess at tennis,
returns your serve with a perfectly executed forehand
    diagonally to the far corner
and you return
                and so does he
                        and so do you.
It is one of those rallies that seem as if they could go on
    for ever.
But you are playing against a metronome.

Sooner or later your concentration will go.
The ball will skid off the racket frame
or you'll slash it impatiently into the net,
suddenly losing your desire to win.

You forget why you were playing.
Your heart is no longer in it.

There are any number of ways of losing a point, careless
    or otherwise.
And Death just waits there, shifting easily from one foot
    to the other, your opposite number,
cool in his shirtsleeves with all the time in the world and
    out of it.

Couldn't you just give up and resign as players do in chess,
admit defeat and live to fight another day,
and go off friendly and have a cup of tea together?
Death doesn't do tea.

So there you are playing tennis, a game you never cared
    for, as if your life depended on it.
And it does.
And the game seems endless.
Yet end it must.

WATCHING TV WITH MY MOTHER

We're watching TV,
a weekday night, the usual fare.
Her lips move as though
mouthing a silent prayer,
but she's not talking to God
or to herself, but to the BBC,
talking back to it, or sorting out
what it's all about:

a pop star's sudden fall
in a drugs-related case,
the latest paedophile,
a minister's disgrace.
The young, their empty lives,
or a serial about strange wives.

The figures on the screen
are like a carousel where
ponies go jingling, toy cars honk,
nothing she recognises until –
is that her grandchild riding past
with a big glad wave?
Or are they just the shadows
on the wall of Plato's cave?

'Oh! there,' she says, 'that must
be dear old Andrew Marr –
he looks younger by the day,
smiling from ear to ear.'

And then another blur
proves to be Tony Blair
and next to him, his wife –
'they're such a ghastly pair.'

And: 'Isn't that John Cleese –
do you remember that boarding house
in Bude? I think he owned it.
He always makes me laugh –
and who's that looking up at him?
It must be Manuel. Oh! look,
he's spilt his tray of meat
and gravy on poor Fawlty's feet.

So like our waiter down the hill
in the Italian.
I always call him Manuel;
I don't suppose he minds.'
She shrieks with mirth,
'I hope I'm not unkind.'

And so the figures whirl and waltz
across the screen like dancing flames,
it could be Westminster or some old *noir* –
in many ways they're rather similar.
Dalziel and Pascoe, Hercule Poirot,
or Inspector Morse of course:
some don's had poison in his soup,
and down they go
like ninepins in a row,
an everyday event, or so it seems –

in academe they do not stoop
to low plebeian means.

Or David Attenborough appears,
bottom upward in the scrub,
raising a finger, winking sly
to ask my mother please be quiet,
as he pursues some furtive species,
hopelessly camera-shy.
Or is he beckoning her in
to his home behind the screen?

It's all a bit too much
when your eyes aren't what they were
and your hearing-aid's mislaid;
did you leave it in the loo –
these things can wander by themselves –
or under the cushion on your chair?

The TV like an eyeless stare
outstayed her by a year, athwart
the room like some demanding idol
or work of modern art.

'You always worked so hard,' she'd say,
'but your sister…she was the star.
She was cleverer by far.'
'Yes, mum, and isn't it time for bed?'
'Oh! no, it's so nice to have company.
I could go on talking hours,' she said,
an unearthly glint in her eye
like a sunset passing by.

NEW PLANS

for Remco Campert

I dreamed that work had begun
on the Leidseplein,
a new master plan for the city.
The Stadsschouwburg has been pulled down
and the Edwardian façades opposite
where a certain bank was housed
pushed over like a house of cards.
A muddy trench runs the whole length
of the pavement cafés on the Kleine-Gartmanplantsoen
where the tourists sat over beer or coffee.

Everywhere
bulldozers and fork trucks. One mighty crane
lording it over ruin.

They are building, a passer-by tells me,
the north-south metro line to Cologne.

The historical city
is about to become history.
Everything must go!

The clearance area stretches as far as Jan Luykenstraat.

And there,
like a cross-section of a doll's house – amazing! –
from the little corner where the theatre bookshop used
    to be,
I can see your house.

They had to draw the line somewhere.
A poet's house stands for ever.

Cat looking out of the window, licking his paws.
An ordinary weekday afternoon.

And your paintings are there, still on the walls,
and your books. In the dream I can read the titles:
Paul van Ostaijen and Jacques Prévert,
the underground line of poetry.

Deborah by the front door
with a friend visiting.

And you upstairs at your typewriter
with the first draft
of a new poem.

Like Carroll's tortoise, you taught us:
the poet moves slow
but is unstoppable.
You renew yourself.
You get your goal.
You become your poetry
and move on again,
driven restless
by that midnight muse,
who didn't let you down,
who never lets you go.

LADY WITH A LITTLE DOG

In the peppermint-green postmodern interior
of the prescription pharmacy
on the Haarlemmerdijk in Amsterdam,
life dawdles in the slow stream.

The irritable cough of the unwell,
warning potential queue-jumpers,
is the nearest we get
to conversation.

Until suddenly
a beautiful woman comes in,
and silence places a finger
on our gaping mouths.

Did the glass door
slide aside for her shyly?
Or had she simply
passed through it?

With her, a man in his forties,
trim moustache, short, tense with aggression –
her father or some more sugary daddy?
Maybe a rich uncle from abroad,
dapper and disagreeable.
And a black and white terrier,
yappy little bundle.

What was she doing here?
She didn't need medicine –

she *was* medicine,
dispatched by the divine dispensing chemist in the sky.

With her pearl-grey short-sleeved dress,
tanned legs in sandals
and cobalt-blue bag hung from her folded arms,
she came wafted in on the May breeze.

(Over her lip a beauty spot
like a cherry dive-bombed by a blackbird.)

She stopped my breath,
unravelling the rigmarole of my thoughts
and getting me in a tangle
of quite a different order.

Her lapdog was an embarrassment
in that clinical space,
so she tipped it into the arms of her *compagnon*
to take outside.

He glowered like a thundercloud,
condemned to pass his days
ensuring so adorable a creature
was never out of his sight –
the lady not the lapdog –
though she drew all eyes.

She gave me such a look
that I was lost for words,
like a panic-stricken passenger
looking for his papers without which he cannot fly.

God help me, I thought,
beauty has carried me off
and made bonemeal of me in her boneyard.

The time was ten-thirty on a Tuesday morning,
but beauty doesn't do appointments.
She shows up when it suits,
preferably when you're at the end of your tether with
    sameness,
pulling you out of the sleeve of yourself,
like a newborn baby
shivering with surprise.

Later I found out
she's the daughter of the dry-cleaner
with the shop on the square.
Usually she's hidden behind the rail of coats
in their polythene sheaths.

Had he recognised me
or divined my intentions?
When I came in with my jacket for repair
he gave me such an angry stare.
More compliment than I deserved.

IN THE BERENSTRAAT

for Richard de Nooy

August in Amsterdam is a second winter. Everything shuts down. It's the dead season. Parched grass and lifeless trees. In the parks nature has lost interest in performing its task. The only sign of life is the throngs of tourists, who gaze empty-eyed at the spectacle that was our city. Ordinary existence has fled elsewhere. I am reminded of Rome in 410, sacked by the barbarians who prowled the deserted streets, astonished by edifices they were incapable of interpreting. Our city is pure façade. The only structures that still function have a carnivalesque character, for instance the windows in certain quarters where near-nude women continue to prance and beckon.

Our barbarians are the tourists, who glare at the vestiges of a lost civilization in their attempt to read meaning into a scene that meaning has abandoned. No sooner do I venture out of doors than I am greeted by their questions. What is the way to the Anne Frank House? Or the Casa Rosso? And what is that little statue of the boy?

I tell them that people once lived in these buildings, parties were thrown and dances held. Loud music poured from the cafés like a torrent of lava. People fell madly in love or betrayed each other in cowardly fashion. Unsolved murders were legion and corruption was endemic, but none of this threatened the vibrant commercial life of the city. On the contrary, these acts of villainy were woven seamlessly into its texture.

Like the ghosts in hell clustering around Dante, eager to hear the latest titbits from the upper world, these tourists listen to my tale. Only it is I who am the ghost and they, no matter how much their behaviour conforms to their type, are the real people.

I am standing here in the Berenstraat, the Bear Street, close to the once pulsating heart of the dead city. I am a native and survivor and this lends me an air of authenticity, so that I am both perfect guide and easy prey for visitors. If they only took the trouble, they wouldn't need me to tell them, but it must comfort them to hear the sound of a human voice in this desolate scene. Here, I tell them, is an artists' bookshop loved by the avant-garde, while further up is an 'ecological' butcher selling meat from livestock slaughtered with great respect. A few steps on and you come to a boutique with the delectable name of 'Parrot Fashion'. A skeletal staff keeps these premises open but essentially, I tell them, what they are viewing is archaeology.

The tourists look at me in disbelief as though I am pulling their leg. Dutifully however they take out notepads and ballpoints. A girl from a mid-west art college is ready with her sketchbook. And later my photo will be peered at by family and friends on home computers from Osaka to Bloomington, Indiana. Who do they think I am? Well-tolerated local eccentric or skunk addict? In any case I am worth a photograph. And on each photo hangs a tale. Like a key on a key ring.

DEAD POETS' QUARTER

After he died
they named a street after him.
A brief ceremony.

His ex-wife
did the right thing
and put in an appearance,

as did a handful of friends,
drunk and unhappy,
and some neighbourhood kids,

their game interrupted,
and their dog,
a forlorn little mutt.

A couple of former mistresses
hovered on the edge of the gathering,
keeping a weather eye on each other.

And, like them, the weather was wintry,
so proceedings were
held to a minimum

with a few words
from the chairperson
of the local arts department,

'He did so much for poetry.
He made it accessible
to ordinary people,'

which was more
than could be said
of the street,

one of a series
of gaps between houses
in a new development

at the end of a bus route
where the grey blocks march
in the middle distance,

given names
to guide the visitor
through the grid-plan maze.

They'd run out of explorers
and nineteenth-century statesmen.
so they dubbed it 'the poets' quarter'.

It was the turn of the poets.
Surprised at so much attention,
they turned in their graves.

One of them
was even overheard muttering,
'It's almost worth being dead for.'

THE WRINKLED SEA AS VIEWED
BY THE WRINKLED SEER

From the dizzying height
of seventy years,

like Tennyson's eagle,
I look down on my younger self.

Far below me
a young man

is setting out in life.
Hope fills his sails.

Little fool, I say,
he has no idea.

But then I remember
the joke's on me.

If only I could stop him,
swoop down from my vantage point

of impotent knowledge,
and seize the twenty-year-old brat

I once was
in my disparaging claws.

'If you'd seen what I see,'
I'd ask,

'would you have done things differently?'
And he replies,

'Like it or not
for worse and for better

you are my me.
We are mates for life.

You are the price I paid.'

RETIREMENT BENEFITS

when we're old
we'll lie in bed
half the day

make each other
feel good

that's what we paid those taxes for
all those years

and the children
will forget to come and visit us

still we'll see them
when they want

what bliss
worth waiting for
all those years

OLD AGE EXPRESS

getting older
I move slower

but my life
runs out faster

a paradox
no time

to make sense of it
just grab life by the leg

before it disappears
into the tunnel

cling to it like crazy
my life my love

when I go
all goes

from
Early Morning

(2017)

WINDOWS ON THE WORLD

Back from Utrecht
on a cold November night,
I realized I'd returned home
without my glasses.

Had I left them on the train?
I cycled through the shivering blast
back to the station.
The lost property office window
shook its head.
Sorry we're closed.

My bifocals,
my second pair of eyes.

They must have slipped from my pocket
when I was cycling home.
I scoured the gutter of the Haarlemmerstraat,
the whole length of it,
like a homeless person
looking for the clue
to where his life took a wrong turn,
when my glasses spotted me.

They were lying in wait
outside the Posthoornkerk
gleaming on the frosty pavement.
Slung loose from their case
which had been squashed by a bike,

there they were on the edge of the kerb,
just fine.

Miraculously reunited with me,
reflecting Cuypers' spires
palely in the lamplight.

Eyes of my eyes,
and windows on the world,
they returned my gaze, vigilant, reproachful:
next time, they chimed,
show a bit more respect for your specs.

Both of us agreed
there's no justice in the world,
only the occasional
bit of good luck.

ROOM WHERE I WRITE MY POETRY

Room of misery,
doghouse,
cynic's kennel,
and the thoughts that will not come,
save images that do a belly flop
or flap like fishes drowned on shore.

Shut up like a selfish monk,
back turned on the world, its joys,
as if despising ordinary happiness,

recording dark stanzas of grief,
afraid of the wide world, its cruel lures.

Sometimes terrified I hit the street
and the street hits back
with noise and carnage,

so I rush back to my wounded den
and compose a diatribe against turpitude
and no poems come.

FRAGMENT

for sumedh rajendran, sculptor

So much waiting
makes the heart pale

breath stutters under the weight
of time postponed

anxiety the hinge
on which our dealings seem to swing

thicker than fear
more layered than dreams

dense clouds
dissolve in tears

yet as the mist descends
it's hard to see

through the fog of war
if in the tent

where their shadows move
indistinct as memory

are they fighting or kissing

CRAWL SPACE

Under the floor in our living room is a crawl space
occupied by a few people gone underground in the last war.
Most of the time we are unaware of them.

They don't need us for anything,
but would they come out anyway?
And if we lift the hatch, they're not there.

Is it because no one told them the war has ended,
or are they expecting a new one to break out?
They are closer to us than yesterday.

Little scuffling sounds late at night may be meant to
        warn us
to keep our ears and eyes open
and watch what we say.

Their almost-heard voices are like hair rising along our
        spine:
'A war, easily triggered, is difficult to stop.'
Or: 'Careless talk costs lives.'

Wise before the event,
we tell ourselves
to stay vigilant.

Not to relax.
Our floor is their ceiling.

SHORTER THAN I THOUGHT

I dreamed that death
has a tailor's shop in Hackney.

I ask him for a bolt of cloth
to measure me for a suit.

Pleased to have my custom,
tells me he's kept busy these days.

No matter, he has plenty of assistants
and recession is boom time for him.

His business expands
as other tailors close.

Perfectionist,
never misses a stitch.

'Has everything sewn up' –
that's his motto.

He takes my measurements.
'That'll be it. You're 5 ft. 8.'

'I thought I was taller,' I say.
'I'm known,' he replies,

'for cutting down to size.'
And, snapping his fold-up ruler closed,

he gives me one of his
clenched, trademark smiles.

'Long or short,' he says,
'is something I decide.'

PUSHING THE ENVELOPE

Who put us in one in the first place?
Did we choose this disguise?
Our poor bones as we were squeezed through the letterbox.

In the dark of the letterbox
I broke
free of the envelope.
Words I spoke,
words of prophecy.

Multitudes of other envelopes simultaneously burst open.
A sound of envelopes rubbing together
like footsteps sliding over melting snow.

I saw a world
where nobody was a dead letter
or needed returning to sender.
Or rewriting.

SWEET MUSE OF POETRY

Muse of gentleness,
of gaiety and laughter. A small hint from your eyes,
was enough for me to fall for you,
like the tower of a child's building blocks
that a tug at a carpet hem may bring down.

This is the tower, this early morning.
Nothing stirs in the house.
Outside there's the thunder of Saturday's garbage round;
otherwise the stillness is uncanny. It's early
in January. The day
can't make its mind up whether to begin.

Muse of my heartbroken heart:
I have no choice but to fall asleep again or write
and I can't get back to sleep.

OUT OF SORTS

In the dumps, can't write, out of sorts.
Look down at your feet.
Look at all that gravel
glistening in the late afternoon shower.
Each stone different,
little individuals.

Tufts of grass in between
and the cat out there stalking a trembling bird.
It's a small world.
It's all there is and it's all there, yet you're not in it.
You've subtracted yourself from it,
refuse to take part.

And now the evening light, transparent lilac.
The sun's out again. The big cloud
is pulled to one side, behind the trees, like a curtain opened.
The sun is shining on your self-stoked despair.
How can you turn down its smiling invitation?

TOILETTE DE FEMME

I am watching you as you do
whatever you do to yourself
in the mirror – 'things,' I say,
'a man never fully understands.'

'Some see more than others,'
you say. 'Others just stare
and don't take in.'
'So which am I?' I ask

redundantly. 'A woman
has to feel right,' you say.
And 'it's no use telling me
I look great already.'

There are your breasts and
the high arch of your behind.
'That,' I say, 'is inarguable;
it cancels out my normal mind.'

Till through the window I hear
the roar of the morning
train to Brussels, +/–
150 passengers on board.

It reminds me of myself,
whoever that may be.
I clear my throat
and start my day.

ARNOLD TALKING

Head propped up with pillows,
his face *en profil* as he speaks to me,
translucent like an alabaster low-relief monument,
only the bent nose suggesting a third dimension.
Pale elongated fingers.

'I don't care for nurses,' he lisps.
'They're a team,
five or seven of them.
They show up two at a time
in all possible permutations.
When they dress my wound
or put ointment on my bed sores,
their prattle is unbearable.'

Later, after a morphine-induced doze,
'I don't care
for BBC 4 either.
The broadcasters must all
come from Sussex or –
a sly glint in his half-open eye –
even Berkhamsted.'

For someone in normal health
such petulance
would be intolerable,
but his vexation
is breaking on shipwreck.

Yet when the nurses do show up,
it's with a no-time-for-chat breeziness.
He informs them,
perhaps unsure of our connection
or fumbling for a formula to account for me:
'this is Donald, my brother-out-law.'

BLIND SIDE

Did you see the accident?
It must have been a bad one. The bike,
its front wheel ripped off, the rest –
you could still just see it was a woman's bike –
flung across the road.
A beige and orange breakdown vehicle, its motor running,
and the usual chaos of police and ambulances.

A chemical smell of casualty
staining the bright dew-filled February morning.

She must have been zipping ahead as the lights changed
when the truck turned right, blindsiding her.
I was off to the park on my morning run but
the accident was an iron hand clamped round my heart,
a magnetic field yanking me back. Later,
to the man putting on his blades at the park entrance:
'it's no fun cycling in Amsterdam any more.'
His blank expression stops me in my tracks.
Another shouty idiot? He's off and away.

STEEP YEARNING CURVE

Your voice is a flower
long-stemmed –
a lily voluptuous and alone.
Or is it a rose
almost purple in the evening gloom,
a splash of blood
against my living-room wall

in a late afternoon in late February
when the days also begin to
turn their heads towards the sun?

Your voice is a flower
tremulous and
quivering with thought.
A deep red flash,
deeper than deep
in the sombre light.

Not a brash sunflower,
looming like a yellow loudspeaker.

Or any little forest blooms,
no matter how darling –
anemones, primroses, bluebells, all serried ranks.

An iris maybe, thrusting upwards,
big mauve tongue, a morning flower?

The voice, *la voix humaine*, essence of being human.
Yes, I know birds sing
but do they really speak?

And I think of how the Dutch word for voice
is 'stem'.
And I think
Of the slender shaft of your throat
And your head with its mass of curls.

I don't need to look
for any other flower.

APRIL IN AUGUST

Two books of poetry came through the post,
unexpected.
They were like troops sent to relieve a city,
one a chapbook, the other
a full volume.
The pamphlet in particular made me laugh
with its witty imagery.

It was as though they had come to relieve the siege of me.
I had become a citadel of self-loathing.
I looked on my works with despair.

Everybody said it – I was my own worst enemy.
I was in a state of unholy deadlock and had thrown away
       the key.
I had laid siege to myself
and lived for years on crumbs of difficulty.

It was an August afternoon of an aching freshness
and a light early-Renaissance breeze,
the grass and trees still green
from the rain of the past month and the birds
filling the sky with their clamour.
It might have been April all over,
the threshold of Spring.

How is it that one voice can release another?
Poetry is not the solitary way I had thought.
When we write we enter a peopled domain.
Only when I let go of myself was the siege lifted
and I was free to write
what I had long had in me.
What I had always wanted to say.

IN DONADEA

An orchestra of birdsong
with a cacophony of crows as backdrop
and the cat out there in the evening sun
taking it all in,
turning her head each which way,
more music-lover than hunter
now her hunting skills
are on the wane.

(Does she dream of her young days
when no little creature was safe from her?)

And through a gap in the hedgerow
the last light falls
on the field with sheep cropping the sweet grass.
Even their backs are shining.

As for me, I'm sitting outside on the terrace
watching the cat watching the birds
and the wind, which has picked up now it's sunset,
is reading the folder of poems in my lap
at a fierce lick,
strewing my pages across the flagstones.

Hasty critic,
no time to waste.

HARE TODAY

There she is
on our lawn this morning,
giving my heart
a jump start.

Cropping the new grass,
ears tipped back,
then a sheer leap,
like a jack-in-a-box,
and – hearing my camera click –
a pirouette
and off she whips
at a faster lick
than this morning's gale.

The wind is racing to catch up.
Our feral cat is no match.
A god has plummeted in our midst.

WAYLAID BY NOSTALGIA

On holiday in Rome,
waylaid by nostalgia,
I said let's go to the writers' café.
It's just round the corner,
Rosati's, Piazza del Popolo.

Alberto Moravia and Elsa Morante
used to sit there,
glamour couple of the 1950s,
and Pier Paolo Pasolini swung by.
Once I saw Tennessee Williams
with a young flame
screech to a halt before the tables in his Maserati,
fresh from the festival in Spoleto,
his gaze raking the café terrace,
white suit blazing in the six-o'clock sun.

Today, forty years later,
the café has a clean scrubbed look,
plenty of gleaming chrome.
Cloths draped over their folded arms,
the waiters stand at the entrance,
making sure that the customers
get a good wait for their money.

The latter rather thin on the ground –
just a few of the not-so-young
looking a little lost
and a handful of backpackers,
heads in their guidebooks
that tell them something
about where they are sitting.

Nowhere a writer in evidence.
'Although,' I say,
'what does a writer look like anyway?
Would you know one if you saw one?'

THE YELLOW BUTTER DISH:
A FOUND POEM

'When I went abroad at Christmas
I left my house to friends to look after
they made hay while the sun shone,
and havoc when it rained,
living in all the rooms at once.

Some days later one of my lodgers phoned apologizing.
She had dropped my butter dish
and felt she had to tell me. What she didn't know
was that the dish she was referring to
was an object of serene but restrained beauty,
dating from 1912, pale yellow in colour.

The lid had a knob to lift it, shaped like a daisy.
I don't know if it had much value, but for me
it was irreplaceable, a sweet treasure.

She hadn't thought to glue the pieces together,
but threw them in the rubbish bin.
Clearly she hadn't heard of the Japanese tradition
by which broken objects are glued together
and viewed as having extra value.
Let alone the Chinese approach where the cracks are
    sealed with gold.

She'd made up for breaking the dish, she told me,
by buying me a brand new whistling kettle,
as mine no longer made an adequate sound.'

AMSTERDAM AUBADE

From our bedroom window in the morning light
Amsterdam's packed façades look brittle like an array of
    doll's houses,
as if cut from cardboard. You'd think
these towering mercantile fronts might fold together like
    praying hands.
As if these tall narrow houses with their pouting
    gable-tops
were so improvised a structure, so delicate and frail,
they might suddenly concertina together
under the late February sun as it climbs resolutely into
    the sky.
Like a book snapped shut, end of story, end of time.
Journey complete, solution to every issue
in keeping with the Dutch ideal of *maakbaarheid*
that translates literally as 'makeable' and means
that you concentrate on what you can do, not on what
    you might dream.

But you and I have another take on the possible,
closing the curtains on the brilliant morning,
folding inward towards each other like praying hands,
watching each other's eyes for the signs of pleasure
and telling each other that there are plenty who would
    tell us
we have better things to do,
things we ought to be doing in the world of the feasible,

the world of doing and of making,
the world of making do.

All these other things may be better but
none are as good as this.

New Poems

(2017–2020)

SUDDENLY IT IS EVENING

ed è subito sera
SALVATORE QUASIMODO

i

Someone asks me
what it's like
being old.

Do you really want to know?
Or are you just making
conversation?

First the good news:
I'm only seventy-
five. My battlements
are not yet crumbling.

Shall I continue?

ii

Like the weather today,
it's not so bad.
September, the threshold of autumn.
Grey, cheerless, but at any rate
it's not raining and there's
almost no wind.

It could be much
worse. Less and less

to look forward to.
Are you still listening?

iii

The days
go by like trains,
I just failed to catch
or else
they no longer
stop at my stop.

I sleep
afternoons, but
the nights are endless.

iv

Or imagine
you're sailing along, almost
becalmed, a serene sky,
when suddenly a cyclone,
some underlying
unsuspected condition
whips up out of nowhere,
leaving you with
the vestiges of yourself,
wreckage dispersed
over a sleepy ocean.

C'est la vie,
or so they say.

And before you know,
it's time to go.

v

Even regret for
everything I didn't do
becomes a lullaby.
Or a cradle where
all my memories rock.

vi

Memories
good and bad,
jumbled up together

one mix:
indifferent.

Do you have
any more questions?
If not, please leave
and close the door after you.
Gently, please! Don't slam.

MINDLESS VIOLETS

When the spring comes
(not today luckily
with the rain pouring
nonstop)

there'll be
a whole horde of them

looking for nothing
to do

BIRDS

All the poetry that could be got out of them
has been written.
Yet they still fly.

That they are descended from us —
little-known branch
of evolution theory.

A blackbird on the path
looks at me quizzically.
The stories she could tell.

SNOWDROPS AND DAFFODILS

A day in early March,
although it might be May
it's so warm,
even in the shade. Legs
splayed under sidewalk tables.
In the park
snowdrops and daffodils blooming together.

Spring comes in a tight package now.
One perfect day
followed by weeks of
hurrying clouds, high winds
and downpour, then,
just as suddenly,
the dustbowl of summer.

Everyone streaming outdoors
all at once.
Spring came as if ordered.
And went.
I wasn't ready for it.

DERRYCRIB

There's not much beauty here.
It's off the tourist routes and
bungalows are mushrooming
for a new breed of commuter.

Not much beauty, except
when the veils of the morning
are still hanging low
and I see from our bedroom window
a green hill.

No mountain, that's for sure –
still it lifts its head
above the morning vapours,
while the horses in the field opposite
graze between drifting shrouds.

Half-past six, I tell you,
(your face half-hidden under the blankets)
and the world holds its breath.

And there's beauty here enough
for those who care to see it,
for those who stop a moment.
For those who stay around.

CRIMINAL NEGLIGENCE

Criminal,
I let myself grow old. I
didn't keep an eye on myself.
Too busy, endlessly busy,
this thing and that, negligible
matters of trivial significance.

I've been failing myself.
My teeth are an own goal, my
eyes weepy, I falter
when I walk. All this
happened
when my back was turned.

If only
I could forgive myself long enough,
maybe I could get a reprieve
from the falling axe of winter,
get some spring back in my step.

POETRY AS THE LAST LUXURY.

Or is it an eye-teaser, a mirage, a vision
like a hind by a pool?
You see the pool
deep in the forest, an empty scene.
And suddenly there's the hind,
nostrils quivering, all watchfulness,
as if that's what the pool needed
to complete it.
It's as if it had been there all the time,
and the next minute – vanished!
And you wonder,
'have I been seeing things?'

BALLAD OF THE NIGHTMARE CAFÉ

My Dutch bank, barely recovered from bankruptcy,
has special offers on its website
for reduced admission to the September exhibition of
   'Van Gogh'.

250 reproductions of the artist's paintings are on show
at Berlage's Stock Exchange building on the Damrak,
with some of the paintings, it warns, 'actually coming
   to life'.

On the café terrace outside, as favoured customer,
you may sample a glass of pastis,
apparently the one-eared artist's favourite tipple.

You may enjoy a pelting from the Potato Eaters,
or join in the conversation at the Night Café
where the regulars will tell you in no uncertain *argot*
what it is that makes this louche bar their favourite
   haunt.

YOUNG

you had
all the time in the world
for what you wanted

only you didn't yet know
what that was

time wasn't yet a deposit account
with a maximum withdrawal limit

IN THE WESTERPARK

On the benches near the
red-brick
former local authority office building,
in the Westerpark,
the winos meet
for beer and conversation

under the bare branches
of an early spring.

Two of them are sitting
at a concrete drum-shaped
picnic table

under the quiet rain
of an early morning.

One of them
is propping his head with his hands,
elbows on the table.
Big heavy
thinking cap on,
he broods over the tabletop
as if deciding the right move
on an imaginary chess board.

What is a life?

His companion,
stiff rain-soused jeans and leather jacket,
is leaning away from the table,
holding up his smartphone and
gazing at it at arm's length.

Perhaps there's an answer there.

A REVENANT

(Nick Leslie, storyteller)

How often after his death
I have seen him,
a revenant

crossing the humpbacked bridge over the Prinsengracht
or peering through the window of the Moroccan
    butcher,

who when he lived carried all before him,
wearing his jester's cap wherever he went.

Falstaffian storyteller,
people gathered around him
as if he was a tree providing shade.

A few months earlier
I had seen him on a small stage in Amsterdam,
a try-out of his new one-man show.
No hint then
he'd soon be gone.

Even now, years after,
when my eye is off guard,
there he is, still strolling the canals,
his figure like a big 'O', his Roman profile,
but light-footed as a somnambulist,
as though there was something that kept him
from bedding down in death.

Or is it more
that I'm the one with something to work out?

Conversation
broken off in mid-sentence;
the gesture
brought down in flight.

I'm pushing my own boat out now,
my little craft of poetry,
into darkening waters.
Waves rolling towards me
from beyond the horizon.
White foam bearding the midnight sky.

DEATH AND TAXES

It was as if she'd died in paperwork.
The pension fund to close. Some creditors,
their final bills. Running accounts
to be reined in, their gallop stopped.

No matter which way you cut it,
bureaucracy attends the dead.

I read somewhere how they do it in the Deccan,
in India. The old stumbling off into the stony hills
taking their last rest under the beating sun,
letting the wild beasts sort their bones.

Not our tradition. It wouldn't be allowed. Besides,
where in the Chilterns
could a dying person hide?

So here's my mother on her final day.
An oxygen mask, six patients in a ward –
a screen drawn round her bed.
She smiles bleakly to help me feel at ease.
Fear in her eyes. Her final words,
whispered in my ear,
'How warm your hand is.'

And all at once there are documents to sign,
lawyer's fees to be paid, while the inland revenue
pours its requirements like wet cement
into the void the loved one leaves behind.

HARDLY NEWS

It's hardly news to anyone
with eyes to see
that the end of the world is at hand.

The signs have long been there,
but we still have to eat
even if the food tastes of nothing,

so we made ourselves make something,
fried potatoes, some salad leaves,
no dressing, and a bit of fish,

its provenance unknown,
sell-by date yesterday.
The supermarket

was clearing its stock,
uncertain there'd be
any fresh deliveries.

Not what you'd call appetizing,
so we gobbled it down
in a hurry, anxious

not to be caught out
by the end of the world
with our mouths full.

OVERSPILL

Late in your life you catch yourself loitering
in the corridors of useless knowledge.

The mind, finding no safe harbour,
seeks shelter in
a snowstorm of forgetting.

Or else
you set about decluttering,
getting rid of
all you no longer need.

Making space
for emptiness.

Travelling light
for your journey
into the sidelines.

What does a person need anyway?

No choice but forward,
like a ship inching through pack ice,
as the floes close in behind it,
in the hope of reaching clear water before nightfall.

MEMORY

What's memory
but the impression
of a thing
after it has passed?

The cat has
leaped from the cushion,
plopped onto the floor
and whizzed off to the bushes.

All that's left is
the cushion's memory
of the plump form of an old cat.

The cushion is impressed,
but the cat has moved on.

IN THE CAFÉ WITH FRIENDS

A. tells me
her friend B.
(carefully disguised as a violinist)
is really a psychiatrist
of the sadistic persuasion.

He sits with us,
smiling like the cat
that's had its fill of cream.
But I'm the one that buys the rounds.

She tells of her girlfriend the dancer
who 'didn't want it enough'
and ended up as a proud, single mother.

Somewhere poetry is around,
the thing I want to want enough.

Elusive, mysterious,
nobody's sweetheart.

I feel the swish of her robe
outside, passing the café window,
leaving a veil of rime on the wintry trees,
and my own breath falters.

OLD WORK

i

Here's Sisyphus
pushing his stone uphill

one last time,
so he supposes.

Grown old,
pushing his rock

of identity, tongue-
tied to a stone,

as if it were
pushing him.

Too old to die,
that's my kind
of immortality.

ii

Language too is a stone,
a weight on the tongue.

Make it new,
Pound said.

All very well, but
it takes

a lifetime
to sing an old song new.

And Albert Camus said,
Sisyphus is smiling.

More a grimace,
say I,

the strain showing
in his face.

Uphill climb
one more time.

Don't give up ever,
or if you must,

give up with abandon.
Give up big time.

POETRY IS PAINTING

Poetry is painting
only more ambivalent

cannot decide
what it will look like

speaks an image
instead of showing it

betrays more than
it portrays

leaves everything
to the imagination

like a field of battle
where desertion receives

the highest accolade.

SNOWBALL EFFECT

Shaping ourselves,
shaping the world.

Making choices,
how to live.

How important it is
to be ourselves.

How we push our world forward
like a big snowball

melting as it grows.
Our lives, our delusion.

There must be a meaning.
We hope to leave a mark

before we enter
the final dark.

While the wind travels
all the while

from nowhere to nowhere,
invisible, save in its effects:

a tree blown down somewhere.
The long grass heaves.

DAYMARE

Putting things away
in my living room or
doing a bit of
washing up – or
strangling the neck of the rubbish bag
with a piece of string
to put outside for Wednesday's collection,
or searching through my shelves for a book
I hadn't looked at for twenty years
and that didn't much interest me
then either.

I felt my powers ebbing
like water draining in a choked-up sink.

And yet
at the end of a rainy afternoon
the key turned in the door.
First your hands round my eyes, blindfolding me.
Then your arms around me as I sulked,
till I found my lips seeking yours.

And I came back like a swimmer,
stroke after stroke,
from a far place
amidst the tossing waves.

SCHEVENINGEN SONG

I lean against you
like a sail heaving with the wind
while the waves roll out like a typewriter carriage,
the sea ticking its endless message,
a single line of poetry
along the whole length of that long beach
with the unpronounceable name.

You are my beacon in the breakers.
I was the wary one.

But if I let you fly from my hand,
like a seagull battling against
a full wind from the sea,
how would I ever know
would you come back to me?

THE WHITE COCKATOO

We're in the station restaurant in Amsterdam
that looks out on platform two.
It's the scene of our first date.

The white cockatoo is still there
after twenty years,
on its perch by the bar,
looking like a bird that's seen too much.

We come here for the *art nouveau* interior
and the romantic *angst*
of a railway station grand café.
Hardly for the service,
though that has a certain
entertainment value.

That first time
our *magret de canard* arrived cold
after forty-five minutes,
as if they'd had to embalm it.

Yet we hardly noticed the delay,
holding hands across the table, and I thought
isn't this wonderful.

But today I'm looking out of the window,
where a train is just leaving
and it is as if the restaurant is pulling out, not the train,
leaving the platform of certainties and a secure life.

Just then
the cockatoo flaps on its perch
and utters a cry
like a guard's whistle,
and I stand up and wave
at the station we are leaving,
and at past and future at once.
And then I sit down again.

And you give me that old-fashioned look of yours
I first saw
twenty years ago.

LITTLE WEIGHT

A tortoiseshell butterfly
keeps flying back to
one pink aster

it can't resist.
Its little weight
still seems enough to shake the flower.

An afternoon in late September.
Unseasonably warm, but
what's seasonable now?

And it could have been
the early autumn breeze
that lifted the flower's skirt
in a rude gust,

while the butterfly
leaned there
into the flower
riding it motionless.

MY BEST ITALIAN

The hardness of that southern face,
that arm thrown across

the open door of the 101 bus,
Palermo, Stazione Centrale.

The man had such an air
of authority, I thought

he was the conductor
barring my way.

Meanwhile his accomplice
was dipping his hand

in my pocket,
all the time in the world.

He might have been
a small-time mobster on TV,

but this was life,
nothing virtual about it.

Only when the bus got going
down the ugliest street in Palermo,

did I realize
I was missing something.

'*Ladri*', I shouted in my best Italian,
'*Sono stato rubato*',

and the woman sitting next to my wife,
almost in tears

said she felt ashamed
for her city.

Then the police station
and the kindly cop with the i.d. photos.

'Don't you think',
I whispered to my wife,

'he's the image
of Inspector Montalbano?'

rescuing a good laugh
from the jaws of misfortune.

He gave us a ceramic plaque
as a memento of our visit.

THERE IS HOPE YET

Back in Amsterdam
on an August afternoon,
warm rain falling steadily
like a foretaste of autumn
out of a colourless sky; is this
my forecast?
Waking from a power nap,
I was a powerless
knot of despair.

Later I discovered that
what I thought was
my broken heart
was only temporarily disabled,
so I set it to work like Cinderella
in my unscrubbed
kitchen.

Dinner was a slice
of poached salmon.
An hour later,
looking out of
my bedroom window,
I saw the sky
was the same colour
as what I'd just eaten.

It had to be a sign.

TWO STEPS DOWN

i

Coming out of the Spanish restaurant
on a Thursday evening,
the front door at an awkward angle,
then two steps down,
he missed one and fell
into the stony arms of the street.

A cracked elbow,
and the pain rose to enfold him
like a flame,
as if time held its breath.

All the heat of a July evening,
had been gathered by the dusk
into a silent moment.

ii

Old age has its litanies
of consolation.

The visit to A & E
only took a couple of hours.
Then home in the taxi
and tucked up in bed
with a hot toddy
and a galaxy of medication,

sleeping pills and paracetamol,
the whole shebang;
and he fell asleep, telling himself
it could have been worse.
Things are bound to get better
from this point on.

THE CLIFFS OF MOHER

We did Clare in a day,
as if we'd never
get a chance to return.

But after the Burren
and Yeats's tower,
we arrived too late.

Night had fallen impermeable,
a gloomy vessel
steaming home
without a catch.

Seen through streaming rain belts,
the cliffs were a dim finger
pointing towards an abyss.

On the lip of the precipice,
a carpark, vast
and void of visitors.

Hopkins had his mountains,
his 'cliffs of fall',

but we had a carpark in a theme park,
something to dwell on
in the long night of the mind.

DANTE'S *TERZA RIMA*

How it runs like a ladder down the page
and you as reader
climb down rhyme by rhyme

hand over hand, or
feet reaching for toeholds deeper down
in the dark of the mind.

This is the gulf of memory.
Seen from the squalid ruin of our time,
we are one with our history and

the sombre pulsing of this verse
booms through a mist of years,
warning of hidden shoals.

How after seven centuries it still holds us
like the mariner's skinny eye,
even though our concerns may have moved on.

No certainty you'll come out whole.
Visionary shadows of the great dead
nailed to their fatal flaws.

SHAKESPEARE'S ENDGAMES

The victor proclaims
reconciliation. The healing
of ancient wounds. The vanquished
are nowhere to be seen.

Were they unwilling
to grace the chariot wheels,
like falling flowers?

The obliterating darkness
of old friends locked in quarrel,
blood rimming the sight.

The issues
said to have been resolved
by all those spilled lives
still fester.

Bolingbroke decides
it's time to shed a tear
for Richard
whose murder he had arranged.

EVERY DAY

Every day is a different day.
I tell myself this, to give myself courage.
I'll return to writing – poetry of an eighty-year old.
No disgrace, you do what you can.
Like Goya's painting of the dog. Drowning or swimming?
Or just keeping abreast,
never mind the giant wave looming.

I'm sitting on the Haarlemmerplein in the June sun.
There are children bobbing and weaving between the
        fountain jets
or tilting their faces upward
to let the water explode over them.
I bend over my notebook, putting my trust in words
as a swimmer does in the sea, a new poem:
'Love is the door and love the key'.
Heaven knows what my second line will be.

IN THE DOORWAY

for Aon Shiel

Supposing you were to come back now,
in the clothes you wore when we said farewell.
Supposing you were to rise and speak, tell us of the journey
    you've been on,
or like an old photo in the developing tank,
slowly take on form again,
till finally you're back with us as we'd want you to be.
Supposing our wish were so strong
that you'd be sitting again with us at the table
with its blue-chequered cloth,
the coffee bubbling in the coffee-maker and the chocolate
    cake already sliced.
And you might stand up then and go to the door leading
    to the garden,
open it and strike a match for your cigarette;
and just at that moment the sun also comes out
for the first time in days,
and lights your face and you turn towards us
in the room with your ironic-sweet smile
that seems to say, 'what can you do?' We are sitting and
    waiting
for you to speak, the start of a conversation,
just one of those conversations we always had,
which we would so much like to be having right now.

ONE MOMENT

At the heart of Camus' book,
at the turn where the worst
– the body count, the dread –
takes a turn for the worse,

somewhere around the middle
of his tale of a long,
long pestilence,
there's a moment of timelessness,

of joy gushing down
or welling up –
which way joy?
It is a moment snatched from life,

unaccountable,
when the grey endlessness of everything
is lifted like a damp towel
from the face of a fallen boxer,

and we escape the estrangement
of the supermarket aisles
where the unmasked mingle with the masked,
in bad-tempered communion.

AT MANOR KILBRIDE

I'm hopping from stone to stepping stone,
slick green algae on the boulders
and the foaming stream around.
It's not deep,
but those rocks are lethal.
Late spring, sharp Irish cold.

On the far shore, so I dream,
is a lean saint holding a palm branch
and a Chinese poet, porcelain-white belly, sunk
    in contemplation.
An idealized landscape.

On the far shore
is a muddy footpath
winding past low alder scrub.

Your voice at my shoulder,
'we've forgotten the sandwiches.
We'll have to go back.'

The hardest part is negotiating the turn.

ACKNOWLEDGMENTS

This book includes work from the following published collections: *Peace Feelers* (Café Books, ed. Christopher Logue, 1969), *For the Flames* (Fulcrum Press, 1974), *No Flowers for the Man-Made Desert* (Forget-me-not Books, 1985), *Starting from Tomorrow* (Forget-me-not Books, 1995), *How to Get the Most Out of Your Jet Lag* (Ye Olde Font Shoppe, Newhaven, Ct., 2001), *The Glittering Sea* (Hearing Eye, 2006), *The Wolf Inside* (Hearing Eye, 2014) and *Early Morning* (Grey Suit Editions, 2017). There are also a few early, uncollected poems. The final section of the book consists of recent, uncollected work.

For first publication of some of the poems in this book I would like to thank the editors of the following magazines, online journals and anthologies: *The Poetry Review*, *Ambit*, *3:AM Magazine*, *In the Company of Poets*, *The Book of Hope and Dreams*, *Acumen*, *The Spectator*, *The New European*, *el corno emplumado* (Mexico), *Tamarind* (USA), *Up from the Ruins* (USA), *Longshot Magazine* (USA), *Home Planet News* (USA), *Waterways* (USA), *LiveMag* (USA), *Poëzie is een Daad* (NL), *The Stony Thursday Book*, *Skylight 47* (Ireland) and *Gallerie* (India).

I have had invaluable feedback on the last section of the book from Maggie Sawkins and Mary O'Donnell, both of whom gave it a close reading. My wife, Selese Roche, has read through the whole manuscript, and her advice has always been excellent and to the point.

Finally I would like to thank Peter Jay for his sensitive and watchful work as typesetter for this collection, and Anthony Howell, my publisher, for his consistent encouragement of my poetry over the years.

Donald Gardner was born in London, but has largely lived outside the UK, moving to the Netherlands in 1979. An Oxford graduate, he began writing poetry in the early 1960s, when he was living in Bologna as a Prix de Rome historian. Later he spent some years in New York where he was a lecturer in English Literature at Pace College. His first live reading was at the Poetry Project on St Mark's Place and in 1967, he took the stage at the East Village Theatre, in the company of Ginsberg, Gregory Corso and others. On his return to London, his first collection, *Peace Feelers*, was published in 1969 by Café Books. A second collection followed in 1974, *For the Flames* (Fulcrum). Recent books are *The Wolf Inside* (Hearing Eye, 2014) and *Early Morning* (Grey Suit Editions 2017). Gardner has always been a literary translator, as well as poet, initially of Latin American writers: *The Sun Stone* by Octavio Paz and *Three Sad Tigers* by Guillermo Cabrera Infante. He has also translated many Dutch and Flemish poets and in 2015 he won the Vondel Prize for his book of Remco Campert (*In Those Days,* Shoestring Press). Now in his eighties, he continues to write poetry and to translate other poets and is an acclaimed reader of his own work.

Other books by Grey Suit Editions

Anthony Howell
The Step is the Foot
Dance and its relationship to poetry
£14.99

The Distance Measured in Days
A novel
£14.95

Gwendolyn Leick
Gertrude Mabel May
An ABC of Gertrude Stein's Love Triangle
£14.99

Walter Owen
The Cross of Carl
AN ALLEGORY
Preface by General Sir Ian Hamilton
£9.95

Iliassa Sequin
Collected Complete Poems
£14.95

*We also publish chapbooks by Donald Gardner, Alan Jenkins,
Fawzi Karim, Lorraine Mariner, Kerry-Lee Powell, Pamela
Stewart, Rosanne Wasserman and Hugo Williams*